System and History in Philosophy

SUNY Series in Contemporary Continental Philosophy
Alphonso Lingis, Editor

System and History in Philosophy

*On the Unity of Thought and Time, Text and Explanation,
Solitude and Dialogue, Rhetoric and Truth in the Practice
of Philosophy and its History*

Adriaan Theodoor Peperzak

State University of New York Press

Published by
State University of New York Press, Albany

© 1986 State University of New York

For information, address State University of New York Press,
State University Plaza, Albany, N.Y., 12246

Library of Congress Cataloging-in-Publication Data

Peperzak, Adriaan Theodoor, 1929–
    System and history in philosophy.

    (SUNY series in contemporary continental philosophy)
    Bibliography: p. 159
    Includes index.
    1. Methodology.   3. Philosophy.   3. Philosophy--
History.   I. Title.   II. Series.
BD241.P38   1986   101   85-27679
ISBN 0-88706-273-3
ISBN 0-88706-275-X (pbk.)

Contents

Acknowledgments

The germ from which this book developed was a talk presented to my colleagues when I was chairman of the philosophy department of the Catholic University in Nijmegen (The Netherlands). The sabbatical leave following my chairmanship gave me the opportunity to write the book. The translation from Dutch into English was done by Mary Ellen Petrisko, Ph.D.; the final revision and the typing of the definitive version was done by Angela M. Licup, M.A. Both had a hard time with my stubbornness in revising revisions but conquered it by their skill and patience. Ans Diepgrond typed the Dutch and the first English manuscript. To all of them I want to express my sincere and profound gratitude.

Introduction

Philosophy did not have to wait for the current boom in the theory of science and methodology to question its own presuppositions. To a greater or lesser extent, every significant philosophy has always included reflection on its own foundations. As a radical form of reflection, philosophizing necessarily develops into a metaphilosophy.

One of the problems confronting metaphilosophy is the question of how it is related to other philosophies and metaphilosophies that developed earlier or are still being developed. Ever since the time of Plato and Aristotle, most philosophers have reflected on the theses and arguments formulated or presupposed by other philosophers. Thus, philosophizing has usually included a (partial) history of philosophizing.

The following meditations concentrate on the relation between philosophy and the history of philosophy, as a problem of metaphilosophy. In this formulation, I presuppose that philosophy and its history do not coincide. It is, however, a crucial question whether they can be clearly differentiated from each other. One thesis that I shall defend in the course of this book involves the claim that, on one hand, a self-aware and thorough philosophizing necessarily implies a (partial) history of philosophy, while on the other hand, a history of philosophy without a certain degree of autonomous philosophizing, here and now, is not possible. We can, however, start form the current opposition of systematic, or thematic, philosophy and the history of philosophy because, even if they do form an indissoluble unity, they still, at least, imply two different perspectives from which their unity can be viewed.

In opposing systematic or thematic philosophy and the history of philosophy, we mean (for the time being) to say that a philosopher cannot confine himself to a commentary on thoughts formulated by others, because philosophical thinking implies the responsibility for personal thoughts – which, in a way, are always new.

With regard to the relationship mentioned above, the perspective of this book will be that of systematic philosophy, which is *ipso facto* a metaphilosophy. Thus, we will reflect on history from a philosophical point of view and in a philosophical way. If our reflection is successful, it will result in a philosophy of the history of philosophy, which, as a part of metaphilosophy, is simultaneously a part of every genuine and thorough systematic philosophy. The history of philosophy as a part of the science of history will not be discussed here directly or as such. The ideas defended here will, however, indirectly imply certain consequences for the "empirical" study of philosophical theory.

Chapter I

Is Thematic Philosophy Still Possible?

1. The present-day situation of philosophy

According to the best bibliography of current philosophy,[1] the majority of publications devoted to philosophical topics are *historical* in nature. They deal with the philosophies of Parmenides, Plato, Augustine, Descartes, Kant, Heidegger, and others, but they limit their own comments to summaries or criticisms at the end of the text. Even many of the studies listed under systematic philosophy are historicizing, since they depend on earlier or contemporary philosophy, which they paraphrase or work out in an individual style. Many books and articles give the impression of being old-fashioned because they repeat and translate old ways of thinking. What is the relevance of other studies that, at least at first glance, seem to be original and new?

A considerable number of these studies work on *formally logical* and *methodological* questions. They start from the presupposition that form and content are clearly distinct from each other and that one can think and write without at the same time thinking the contents to which the formal elements apply. Another prejudice that often prevails in this kind of study is the idea that philosophical thought is possible without the knowledge of its past.

A third group of thematic studies consists in diagnosing the crisis in which philosophy finds itself. One ascertains or presupposes a void and meditates on the possibility, or impossibility, of philosophy.

Can we still find philosophers who do not stop at formal analyses or repetitions of the past? Has everything been said, so that there is nothing new to say? Has the time of actual creation passed? Is the ever-increasing number of philosophers in the western world a mere assembly of funeral orators, an international congress of heirs who can speak of nothing else but the riches of their forefathers and the structures that dominated the inherited works of their testators? Are we condemned to repeat our past by translating inherited thoughts into the language of our century, by posing them as possible solutions or explanations to our current problems, or by criticizing earlier elaborations on the basis of old principles and perspectives? Most of the contemporary productions in philosophy look back to a lost era, when it was still possible to be a true philosopher — and not just an expert in philosophy.[2]

Is our picture of contemporary philosophy too somber? New things are happening. It cannot be too late for creation. The development of "modern logic" and the theory of science, for example, seems to indicate a new beginning and to legitimate our hopes for the future. Or, is it correct to say that modern logic does not involve a fundamental renewal of old patterns of thinking but has in fact fallen back into conceptions concerning form and content, reality and possibility, thinking and objectivity, and so forth that have been known and refuted for quite some time? Do not these objectors themselves belong to an obscure and obsolete past? What do they understand by 'fundamental'? At what level are they aiming? What do 'renewal' and 'obsolete' mean? Why is it necessary to be new?

2. Think on your own!

If it is true that philosophy is stranded in a historicizing and formalistic criticism of old philosophies, an initial reaction could be a call for a new beginning. We should try to start philosophy all over again.

Have the courage to think independently about the important questions of existence, world, society, history! It is a shame that philosophers keep hiding behind the pronouncements of their predecessors by referring those who ask them for wisdom to conceptions of a past in which we no longer live. The logical analysis of formal elements is at least a productive activity and a healthy training in skillful thinking. Even if it does not produce new truths because of its formalism, it may turn out to be the best preparation for a future philosophy. In replacing the creative work of thematic thinking with expositions of former systems, we are as sterile as those who talk about music instead of making it.

I wonder, first of all, what this admonition means, and secondly, if it is a good reaction. By asking these questions I am following a tendency of our over-reflective times. I will not let myself be tempted into giving my approval or rejection immediately. First, I want to reflect — by a sort of metaquestion — on the meaning and value of what has been said; in this way I am postponing my reaction to this reaction. Of course, another tendency of our times is to ignore every statement that, like the encouragement quoted above, sounds moralizing and to look at such statements as something of which a philosopher should be ashamed. In the course of this book I shall come back to this issue and its presuppositions. For now, I will abandon myself to a reflection on the significance of the above-quoted reaction.

2.1 *What does this incentive mean?*

An encouragement to independent thinking is suggested, as opposed to an exclusive concentration on the history of philosophy. We ought to dedicate our energy to original thought on philosophical questions that are important here and now. Clarifying the presuppositions implied in this encouragement demands a treatise on the essence and meaning of philosophy and philosophizing. The following points are particularly relevant to the problem that concerns us in this book.

In reflecting here on the nature and characteristics of systematic philosophy, we are not making a choice for a particular conception of philosophizing that identifies philosophy with the construction of a system. Justified articulations and coherence are of course essential for every serious kind of thinking, but these can also exist without the foundations and pillars of an encompassing construction. Genuine philosophy may consist of explorations that open a new area, in aphoristic elucidations of fundamental viewpoints or in fragmentary thoughts testifying to one and the same "spirit," without capturing this spirit in the form of one or more theses. An all-inclusive logic would have to thematize all possible manners of coherence. However, (a) if philosophy has a future, then "all possible manners" are never given, and (b) such a logic would itself be governed by a coherence that it could not think, unless it were totally transparent to itself. But is such a consciousness of thinking, such an "understanding of understanding," possible?

In opposing systematic or thematic philosophy to historical studies, we imply the necessity of asking questions and acquiring insights here and now, with respect to controversial things, situations, relations, and constellations. A philosopher of earlier times may have said many things that we can adopt, after translation and adaptation. In this case, history has helped us. The truth, which it has brought to light, *we now see ourselves.* Once we have seen the truth, we no longer need to study history. Our thought must liberate itself from all conformity to the speech of the past, which has not been, and can never become, our own speech. We must ourselves philosophize! We cannot flee into the roles of mere exegetes and commentators.

With this we arrive at the principle of *autonomy,* celebrated — especially by modern philosophy — as the founding principle of all rational thought. Thinking thoroughly and independently is still the principle that makes philosophy different from all other forms of speaking and thinking. Was it not already so — even if somewhat less manifest — at the beginning of the sixth century B.C.? The opposition of independent thought and philosophical history is merely a specification of the opposition between autonomy and authority. The "ancients," the "classics," the "great philosophers" are necessary masters. But their teachings profess a desire that we, as their pupils, check, criticize, assimilate and transform their thoughts into our own. They prompt us to liberate ourselves from our dependence on them, making us strong enough to defend our insights with our own arguments.

Taking responsibility for a philosophy means that one is not merely a knower or a commentator, but a philosopher. Is it possible to be a philosopher without first entering into an ongoing process of historical thinking, and struggling with it? Is the history of philosophy necessary as exercise, introduction, and preparation for those who want to become philosophers themselves? Or is originality strong enough to start from zero?

I do not know of any philosopher who started from nothing other than his own thought. It has been shown extensively by Gilson and others that Descartes's demonstrations, for example, are full of reminiscences and memories of preceding philosophies.[3] All important philosophers nourished themselves on texts and thoughts that were produced before they started to think themselves. Must this fact not be explained by the impossibility of beginning absolutely fresh — an impossibility characteristic not only of philosophy but also of music, painting, literature, dancing, sports, religion, language, and all cultural activities? Attempts to create something completely new quickly degenerate into primitivisms reeking with affectedness or incompetence. The exhibit of totally white canvasses with which the Tate Gallery regaled its visitors several years ago could not have been set up by a monkey; it had just enough humanness to awaken derision, shame, and fury. Such, also, is the case in philosophy. Whoever believes that he has something completely new to say usually does not know that most of his statements sound familiar to anyone who knows the history of philosophy. Originality is the very personal way in which someone renews the existing, not the creation of something out of nothing — which would be by definition strange and incomprehensible.

It is, however, neither necessary nor possible to know the entire history of philosophy before one dares to be a thinker oneself. In this regard, too, we can begin with the recognition of a few facts. The lifetime granted to the longest-lived person is still not sufficient for the reading and understanding of all existing texts. Perhaps it was still possible for Aristotle to study all the philosophies written before him. His historiographical notes, however, show that he presented the notions and arguments of his predecessors in a typically Aristotelian way. We see something similar in all great philosophers, right up to the present time.

When Aquinas, Kant, Hegel, Nietzsche, and Heidegger rendered what earlier thinkers had said, their own viewpoints and trains of thought were so powerful that their predecessors would have seen their versions as distortions rather than faithful reproductions of their thoughts. Some great philosophers are careful enough not to pretend that they know the whole history of philosophy. Others do indeed make such a claim. Hegel is their coryphaeus. Although it is true that Hegel's knowledge of medieval philosophy is deplorable, it has often been shown that his treatment of Plato, Aristotle, Spinoza, Kant, and others distorted their philosophies by understanding them as the effects of conceptual moments and theses that possess a peculiar meaning and coherence within Hegel's own work. His transformations of other philosophers' thoughts were full of injustices, but they were creative: he produced a new and powerful version of knowledge, at the cost of an old one. The battle waged by philosophers in their rendering of one another's thoughts, however, makes them a family of thinkers. While they sometimes grossly misunderstand one another, they are bound together by the same search for the one and universal truth.

Perhaps it is not merely due to contingent factors such as haste or negligence that independent thinkers fail to do justice to their predecessors and contemporaries. Perhaps there are more fundamental reasons for this injustice.

The thesis I shall defend in this book is that a thinker's most fundamental perspective also determines his study of history. If this is true, we can understand why an original thinker is incapable of comprehending another original thought exactly as it is presented by the other thinker. When he attempts to integrate the other's viewpoint into his own questioning and thinking, he inevitably transforms the other's perspective. The complete openness demanded by the absolute neutrality of an "objective" history is not compatible with the particularity of a philosophical (super)perspective. Does this not exclude the possibility that the historian himself thinks? Can a neutral version of other philosophies be thought by someone who himself philosophizes?

A philosopher's fundamental perspective can change. The fundamental history of thinking takes place at the level of the basic perspectives, and the struggle of a thorough philosopher involves precisely the establishment of an all-determining viewpoint, which he never completely gets in sight but to which his thoughts bear witness. A philosopher, genius though he may be, cannot bend the basic perspectives from which he perceives, suggests, asks, seeks, and speaks to his will. They form a particular character. Within the boundaries of this character, someone's acquaintance with other thoughts and ways of thinking can be fruitful. The greater the space of one's character, the more universal one's philosophy — although all concrete universality remains relative to the individual who thinks it.

The "character" of thinking can explain why it is difficult — perhaps impossible — for even the great thinkers to do justice to other thinkers, great or small. Perhaps we must dare to say that a genuine thinker cannot do full justice to another thinker, because his basic perspective is not merely an(other) instance of the same perspective but a radically different one.[4] This difficulty, however, admits of degrees. Some thinkers are closer than others: their problems, approaches, and styles have an affinity to one another. Such colleagues understand each other more easily than they do thinkers who strike them as foreign. Truthfulness and discovery, however, demand journeying beyond one's own circle. Adventure, exploration, and alienation are equally necessary for fundamental thought. To measure oneself by very different manners and starting points, to fight with great and greater enemies, to elicit criticism — all of these are a necessary counterweight to the cozy familiarity of small spirits. While it is true that one cannot fight all of the others, everyone needs a few enemies of his own. Antipodes can be beneficial. However, some philosophers, influential though they may be, think so differently that they do not mean anything to me. They move along other paths, which surely have their meaning in the culture of which I am a part; but I can only think, and must live, along those paths practicable to me.

The great philosophers did not become great by reading everything written on a certain topic. They conversed with several selected predecessors and contemporaries, in their own individual styles.

The comprehensive study of existing literature needed for a systematic treatment of a topic is in most cases impossible, even from a practical and physical point of view. This is also true in cases where a complete bibliography suggests that such a study has, in fact, been achieved. The myth of a complete study of existing literature rests on a fundamental misconception. Comprehensiveness is not an essential element of philosophical genuineness. Thorough thinking does not presuppose a totalization. Granted that universality is characteristic of true philosophy, it must nevertheless be unifiable with the fundamental perspectivism of the individual. In most cases the claimed comprehensiveness is a lie; in any case, it denies the point of departure of all thought: an individual thinker who struggles through a small segment of systems, fragments, and suggestions.

Can we really identify philosophy, as we have done, with the philosophy of the "great philosophers"? What are "great philosophers," really? How does one become "great" in philosophy? Does it really make sense to speak of "greatness" in philosophy — as one would of composers, generals, and politicians?

All philosophical styles — even the "ahistorical" or "antihistorical" forms of positivism, logical empiricism, logicism, and phenomenology — have their heroes. Even in the sciences, such as mathematics, physics, chemistry, and astronomy, one venerates founders and paragons. A characteristic of their greatness is their originality. But, not all originality is valuable. Something new is not necessarily true or fruitful. What kind of originality is "great"? The value of originality must yield to the criteria of truth and veracity. Aside from this, "greatness" in thinking seems to demand that a thinker offer a vast thought space. This is not necessarily to be taken in the sense of a totalizing integration or a comprehensive view — if this were so, Hegel would be the greatest philosopher on this ground alone — but rather in the sense that one inaugurates a free space, necessary for the full and thorough development of some of the genuine and "great" problems of human existence, of the world, and of history, so that other thinkers can also approach these problems in a new and newly fruitful way. With this statement I am anticipating what is to follow. The question of great and small in philosophy can only be resolved when we know what philosophy is and ought to be. Once again, this is a question of metaphilosophy. For the time being, however, we can content ourselves with an appeal to the difference, generally accepted — even among ahistorians and antihistorians — between great philosophers on one hand and epigones, commentators, and repeaters on the other.

The various categories in the second group build on the foundations laid down by the great and do not renew the grounds of philosophy. A subdivision is possible, insofar as some of these followers devote themselves primarily to paraphrasing and explanation, while others draw the consequences of the doctrines they have received and apply them to the questions of everyday life or science. Both groups are useful. They keep the great philosophies alive and pass along what, without their help, would only be accessible through a time-consuming exploration of the difficult texts left behind. The existence of epigones and exegetes is, however, a danger as well. Their own minds are not as great as the thinkers' to whom they have listened. They subject great thoughts to the limitations of their own intelligence. Consequently, what they pass along are narrow conceptions of the original. A forbidding example of this danger is the idea that Plato divided reality into a heaven full of ideas above and an earth, consisting of reflections, below. The situation becomes worse when a so-called commentator is hostile to a great philosopher. The pedantry of his caricatures is unbearable, especially when he sets the tone in certain milieus. Plato himself had pity for people who inflicted such injury upon their own souls.

Let us return to the questions involved in the encouragement given above. Next to the historicizing manner in which "continental philosophy" and a large number of English and American studies accomplish their reflection, there is a way of thinking that seems intrinsically independent of historical figures and traditions. It has left its teachers and upbringing behind and builds up, out of its own forces, a whole system of thought that can bear its own weight. Others claim that this autarchy is merely appearance and that its dependence on historical decisions, presuppositions, frameworks, and automatisms has simply been masked. But even if those who claim emancipation from predecessors and traditions really think autonomously, their philosophies have a formalistic character, without any content peculiar to them. They find substance in the opinions of common sense, in the positive sciences, or in the subjective emotions of anyone venturing a new opinion. This sort of philosophy expresses itself most purely in "modern logic." Although many of its practitioners believe it is the only scientific form of logic, it is neither the only possible nor the only serious one. "Modern logic" *is* scientific, but is it profound enough to be a philosophical discipline? Does it not come all too spontaneously from certain preconceived, unanalyzed, and uncritically transmitted notions with respect to "reality," "form" and "content," the relation between thinking and reality, between rules and applicability, quality and quantity? Does it not begin with notions typical of a specific time-honored ontology, which precedes and follows the theory of thought and thinking presupposed by this kind of logic? When one establishes a formal logic independent of the rest of philosophy and its history, which presuppositions are made and which problems are solved without being posed?

It is very important that we state, once and for all, the usefulness, necessity, and fertility of "modern logic" as it has been, and is now, practiced in close connection with the principles of mathematics. The acumen invested in it, and the struggle for clarification waged within it, deserve admiration and praise. It is, however, just as important to state that the questions *preceding* the separation of form and content can neither be asked nor answered by logic alone. In order to ask and answer these more fundamental questions, we need to confront formal thought with reality — to which purely formal thinking supposedly "applies" — and with other forms of thought.

Logic is preceded by an onto-logic that is, simultaneously, a logic of logic. If one of the conditions of philosophy is thoroughness, then those who deny that the name *formal and transcendental logic* implies a meaningful problem or those who scorn the best books on this topic cannot be considered philosophers.

The necessity and value of modern logic cannot be justified by the supposed fact that it is the only, or comprehensive, theory of correct thinking. If logic is indeed such a theory, it must prove this by a transcendental logic that is at the same time an onto-logic, or ontology. A purely formal logic can however be seen as an experiment through which the possibilities of a certain viewpoint, or a fruitful abstraction, are thought and tested. How far can we go? What can we discover *if* we define, analyze, reason or form hypotheses in such a way? What comes to light when we practice *this sort* of exactitude and consistency?

As a rigorous experiment in thinking, formal logic should be seen from the broader perspective of the basic philosophical question concerning the unity of, and the difference between, thinking and reality. Modern logic cannot be a starting point unless one realizes from the outset that its transcendental and ontological conditions of possibility must be thematized *elsewhere* — *before and after* logic. It is not only necessary to respect its successes, but also to qualify its claims, in order to keep modern logic as a philosophical discipline. Without qualification, formal logic degenerates into a science that opposes its own foundations and philosophy. This results in trivialization and the punishment of death by boredom. That, too, has happened before in the realm of thought.

Now that we have formulated some preparatory considerations of this point, let us attempt a definition of 'thematic' or 'systematic' philosophizing, as opposed to the historical treatment of philosophy: it is *a thoughtful consideration of genuine problems on one's own, here and now.*

"Genuine problems" contain naive and transcendental questions of form and content; they differ from apparent problems in that they can truly and justifiably be taken to heart. Problems that we are persuaded to accept as problems cause us to furrow our brows, but we do not really recognize them as problems. Interesting tidbits, puzzles, riddles, facts worth knowing, trick questions, and so forth can function as whetstones for our understanding, but they remain a game. All genuine philosophical questions touch upon the central questions of human life in the world and in history, directly or indirectly. Being absorbed by such problems is one of the characteristics of philosophy: it is always related to what truly and ultimately matters. Logic, the theory of science, and philosophical methodology, for example, show their philosophical importance when their relation to the essential questions of human existence is made explicit.

We must philosophize *here and now.* Genuine problems are questions that we, as unique individuals of this culture and time, can really ask. They are not questions left over from another time, no longer meaning anything to us, nor are they tomorrow's questions, which we cannot even imagine. The actuality of genuine philosophy not only distinguishes itself from worn-out problems and dead theories but also from the *dernier cri*, the fashion, the alleged "matters of fact" and "historical attainments" celebrated by semi-intellectual, intellectual, and quasi-philosophical groups and congresses. Whether old or recent, all such authorities and prejudices must be examined here and now and, if necessary, amended or destroyed in order to acquire relevant and concrete, but never final, truth. Philosophizing always means leaving the apparent "matters of fact" behind, even when one is concerned with extremely respectable "matters of fact," such as Platonic, Hegelian, Marxist, or phenomenological ones. Emancipation pertains to any serfdom, whether that of "the

Ancients" or of recent pacesetters. In contrast to the tendency to dwell in a beautiful and rich past, another tendency — just as serflike but not always so deeply rooted — is animated by the newness of fashions that do well and receive approval. *Reflection* implies that a thinker reviews both what has been said before and what is now being said. He poses the same question to old and to new philosophies: In view of the insight I desire and hope to win, what is worthwhile in this offer?

The struggle, free from all prompting, to achieve truth is essential to *independent thinking*, on which all thematic philosophy stands or falls.

The thinking of churches, political factions, fashions, and great philosophers, however, has power over the thought of anyone who attempts to think independently. Such power is unavoidable, and not necessarily destructive. Great masters are great, not only through their breadth of vision, depth of insight, or subtlety of analysis, but also because of their desire for followers who will surpass them on pathways of their own. In the face of overwhelming ideas and ideologies, a rebellious reason expresses denial. "Learning begins with criticism . . . . "[5] But emancipation through denial remains either a stammering primitivism, which has yet to learn everything, or a claim that is ignorant of its own dependence. To challenge Thomistic scholasticism with Marxist party ideology, or to replace Platonism with obedience to some form of positivism, does not establish independence. One serfdom is merely replaced by another; fundamentally, one has not advanced beyond choosing this or that dependence.

The idea of emancipation in order to attain total self-reliance in philosophy, however, is itself naive, at least according to most, or all, of the great philosophers after Hegel. The intention of Descartes, who wanted to open the eyes of "the Ego" by unfolding its autonomy, has been criticized and judged impossible by Kierkegaard, Marx, Nietzsche, Freud, Heidegger, Merleau-Ponty, Levinas, Derrida, and others. Preceded by so much obscure reality of a physical, psychical, sociological, cultural, and historical nature, the thinking ego, enlightening itself, will never be able to understand itself totally. An "It" always annoys "Me," so that the "Ego" can never completely attain itself in its thought.

Thinking for oneself is therefore not to be conceived as a practice that commands complete independence. Between the total denial, through which an abstract emancipation rebels against traditions and authorities, and the attempt to build an independent system, philosophers today move in a horizon full of clouds, twilight, and darkness. Even to Hegel, who considered absolute knowledge to be possible, grey was the color of the land where philosophy dwelt. One can contrast his German twilight to the brillance of Greek heavens. But, do not forget the shadows of the mountains!

To think on one's own means to find a thoughtful and sober attitude towards *already existing* philosophies through texts, sayings, popular ideas, traditions, teachers, and discussions; means to be involved, to digest, assimilate, take in, and give out; in other words, means to be a good pupil, who prudently uses the supply of all those prefaces and authorities. Determining which philosophies one must be schooled in is a great practical problem. Initially and temporarily, a pupil is defenseless against the coryphaei presented by his surroundings. Fortunate indeed is the student who comes into contact with great texts and teachers. Who still considers Reinhold, Bardili, Krause, and Keyserling to be great philosophers? Can we be sure that the works of Scheler, Marcuse, Habermas, or Althusser will remain important in fifty or a hundred years?

Aside from the desire for autonomy, the struggle for an independent philosophy involves the acceptance of temporary guidance, and a critical distance, from the leaders who show us the way. Respect and criticism are both necessary for growing into, and outgrowing, one's serfdom. Only a good pupil — that is, one who is neither a slave nor an all-knowing student — is on the way to mastery.

Is it not too naive to presuppose the possibility of thematic thinking, here and now? Are we still capable of developing a philosophy of our own? Has philosophy, in this sense, not passed away?

An endless reflection on the content, meaning, and structure of past philosophies, and on the conditions for the possibility of future philosophies, seems to be a symptom of our times. We live in a culture that is highly knowledgeable about earlier and other cultures.

History and archeology, sociology and cultural anthropology collect enormous amounts of information on events of the past, but we do not actually engage in them. Poetry produces verses about the difficulty, the impossibility, the emptiness of making poetry. Music refers to earlier music. Everything has been said and composed. Doctor Faustus suffers from the impossibility of being original and genuine. We enjoy perfectly restored and reproduced beauty, but we are incapable of bridging the gap separating us from the life manifesting this beauty. Imprisoned in a great and universal Museum, we shrink into a viewpoint that has no peculiar content of its own.

These days, philosophizing seems more like a tour through this museum rather than a production of new thoughts that deserve to be called great. Have we exhausted the possibilities of philosophy? Is there still hope for the philosophers attempting to break down the walls of their mausoleums, or are we doomed by our times to mere outcries of impotence? Formalism, historicism, and scepticism seem to be symptoms of a nihilism that reigns universally, pervading the deepest ground of our questioning.

But is this an irresistible force? Is the autonomy of thinking too feeble to overcome this fate, this *Geschick*? Or, are we, as unresisting souls, prey to a cultural power that simply takes our breath away and paralyzes our wits? Must we wait with patience and expectation?

A comparison with the periods of standstill that occur on the path of life, as described by the mystics, suggests itself. Is philosophy going through a similar transition, in which, through effort and passion, a new fertility is being nurtured out of reflective ignorance? Or does this explanation ignore those domains where it is not mere night and wasteland, but where there are also promise and the beginning of new knowledge?

While its exploitation of old texts and its reflections on past thoughts give a conservative and nostalgic impression, the characteristic way in which part of contemporary philosophy bends back over itself and its past seems to have a future. Its self-reflection expresses itself not only in the paraphrasing of existing ideas but also in the attempt to understand *what saying, thinking, writing, communicating, texts, books, philosophers, history, and culture actually are.* A reflection of this kind can no longer be called purely formal; for when it is done thoroughly, it must necessarily consider the main questions about the essence and the meaning of humanity, society, culture, and history. Thorough reflection on the assumptions of any formalism leads to a philosophy that is simultaneously a thematization of the concrete reality and of its formal elements.

When a formal reflection takes account of the abstractions from which it derives its beginning — and as philosophical reflection it cannot avoid an attempt at this self-knowledge — it is forced to transcend these abstractions, in order to become a theory about the relation between 'form' and 'content' and, thereby, a fundamental philosophy. The realization of this inner necessity, through which a hidden content is recognized in every formalism, is a considerable step in the direction of a new thematic philosophy. Through the explication of the anthropological, cultural, ethical, and ontological moments that the current *Dauerreflexion* contains, new openings and paths, possibly explorable, come into being.

Explication, however, is not sufficient. The manner in which formalism and transcendental thinking occur finds itself in a process of bending and changing which — for lack of ready-made formulas — can only be attempted and experimented with. Must our logic and language be undermined and disrupted before philosophy can renew itself?[6] Or, does a less destructive, more patient way of thinking (and thanking) promise greater fruitfulness?

There is, perhaps, a second reason for judging current ways of philosophizing more positively than was done above. Phenomenology was a new beginning insofar as it — at least *in voto* — made philosophy very concrete for the first time. Its intention was directed at concrete philosophizing about the living, eating, feeling, working, suffering, and communicating of human individuals, their various ways of dealing with one another, and so on. Is the concreteness of this and similar realities compatible with the essence of philosophy? Must thinking undergo a radical change to accomplish this task? Or, is philosophy so dead that it must make room for other forms of wisdom and science?

2.2 *Is this a good incentive?*

The preceding was an attempt to say what the summons to philosophize, here and now, means. At the same time, it was a partial answer to our second question: is the summons a good reaction to the current state of affairs in philosophy?

Can the current impasse in contemporary philosophy be dispelled by courage and strength of purpose? Or does the incentive bear witness to an illusory work ethic? To the ears of those who perceive an ineluctable fate in the Museum of our culture, all such summonses to independent thinking sound moralistic. We are enmeshed in stories long known, paraphrased, applied, criticized, and analyzed. The myths and systems that make the rounds are like old fairy tales, which variation can no longer make more interesting. In spite of this, an appeal to original thinking seems to be futile. It produces, at the most, an appearance of thinking — and, thus, lies.

The virtue of patience does not come about spontaneously, and waiting alone is not enough; after all, good thoughts do not grow on trees but presuppose searching and hard work.

An exercise in productive waiting *can* mean a cautious turning towards the high points of our past. A hermencutical relationship with oldcr philosophies of high caliber can make us well versed in philosophical matters. Through a careful study of Plato, Spinoza, Kant, and others, a kind of philosophical knowledge is developed wherein one learns to be embarassed should one fall back to inferior ways of thinking. The return to our past must be inspired by a feeling for genuine questions, which are never a monopoly of one period of time. A certain kind of atemporality, untimeliness, *Unzeitgemässheit*, characterizes the problems that genuinely and ultimately concern philosophy and, thus, the form of hermeneutics that has a future.

Perhaps formalistic and transcendental reflections can also be practiced in a way that prepares a new possibility for philosophy. A reflective formalism cannot be externally unaware of its own ontological, existential, and historical presuppositions! A thinker will at least ask himself occasionally: What am I doing? What good is my constant concern with forms in this way? A transcendental reflection that does not arbitrarily close off its return to itself is confronted by the question of its relation to the existential and historical ground from which it arises.

Whatever the case may be, courage and patience are not sufficient. Aside from perseverance in working and (a)waiting, there is a kind of thinking that can come to us, without our having the experience of producing it. A name for this was "inspiration." The capacity to think, too, seems to be a fate more gratifying than the stagnation we are suffering; a sort of given (or giving) for which we can hope.

There is still another answer to the question whether the summons to independent thinking is a good one. This answer, too, begins with our imprisonment in "mausoleality." However, it concentrates on our language, which supposedly controls our thinking down to its very core. Before we can think in a new way, we must disrupt and undermine the existing languages. How can we create passageways under and across the established common venues, explode commonly accepted schemas and structures, break with traditional fundamentals, and shake the classical ideas about grounding and formal procedures?

Fundamental questioning likes to express itself in rhetorical terms. Whoever resorts to rational justification necessarily falls into variations of the traditional arguments. It is, then, not surprising that the more combative approach indicated in the preceding paragraph is accomplished by a reevaluation of rhetoric. A certain violence is inevitable, even in philosophy, and is considered "good" — insofar as this word can still be meaningful.

A certain reevaluation of the language of power possibly forms the main difference between this criticism and the classical tradition, which considers rationality to be the opposite of violence. Revolt against commonly held opinions and customs! Is philosophy based on power? Are all concepts forms of conquest? Is truth out of style? Is every thought political? Is philosophy a work of art that can only be loved, celebrated, hated, and despised, but not justified?

Chapter II

Philosophy is Learning

1. Pupil, teacher, text

Just as art, calculus, and speech demand a certain training, so does philosophy. It begins with a learning process: orientation, introduction, digestion of existing thoughts, practice in thinking for oneself, participation in continuous and ongoing philosophical discussions.[7] No one can become a philosopher unless he is led into a philosophical activity, which already has a history. An absolute beginning, not preceded by any instruction, seems impossible. Attempts like this produce primitivisms in philosophy comparable to the groping experiments of certain painters and musicians. But even in such experiments, the historical background that one distances oneself from is not forgotten.

Philosophical instruction can occur in two ways: first, the teacher may develop his own thought and show his student what he ought to think. Second, the teacher may present, explain, and comment on the philosophy of a third party, perhaps that of a greater philosopher. Practical considerations may not allow the pupil to attend lectures of this third party directly. His teacher-interpreter is, then, a surrogate. His commentary might however be more advantageous than the direct instruction of a great philosopher — for example, by being easier to understand. If the third person is dead, the commentator is forced to rely on posthumous texts. The classical texts of philosophy form a collection of great philosophies from which our history developed and which we still honor as paradigms of philosophical thought. In art, too, past masterpieces cannot be duplicated, but we observe them carefully to enable us to produce new artistic expressions of a different kind.

21

The situation is of course more complicated than is suggested here. The teacher may also share a text that he has produced himself. In a certain sense he inevitably does this when he returns to some of his previous statements, or to a former argument. In this respect, preceding lessons are no different from the written texts of a remoter past. As soon as someone has said or written something, he has already left it behind. Afterwards, the author finds it a congealed thought that has become, to a certain degree, strange and alien. He is "confronted" with it, amazed that he said it, content with it, or anxious to deny it. If we may allow ourselves an overstatement, we could say that all speaking or writing is a kind of dying. Once a word is spoken, and in particular a text written, the author is captured and fossilized.

A teacher seldom dares to present his own thoughts by themselves. He knows that his philosophy is neither the only good nor the most comprehensive one. For this reason he goes beyond himself to the best forms of philosophy and takes on the role of guide in the exploration of other philosophies. Under his guidance the classical texts receive preferred treatment, because they are the most authentic expressions of great thoughts. When a teacher paraphrases someone else, there are a number of reasons to doubt the fidelity of his version. Since every epoch knows only a small number of summits in philosophical thinking, the greatest part of great philosophy is embodied in old texts. The important philosophers of our times — not necessarily the renowned names — are active through their spoken words, as well as through their writings. Perhaps there are still Socrateses walking the streets, but their influence outside the immediate circle of their adherents depends on the texts that their Platos write.

In the preceding paragraphs, the difference between talking and writing was merely tied to pragmatic motives: a dead person cannot speak and a faraway philosopher cannot be heard, but they can be read. An oral rendition of philosophical thoughts also differs in a more fundamental way from a written one. The speaker can assist his own (written or spoken) text when it presents difficulty to listeners or when it is misunderstood.[8] He can reply to further questions, consequences, implied presuppositions. In this way he brings the meaning of his text to life, making it (more) fruitful, or even changing it. And with regard to its meaning, the text itself contains all the answers.

A dead philosopher's text can only come to life through a living thinker's recreation, for example, by a thoughtful commentary. On the other hand, a living philosopher has a variety of options regarding the word he has left behind: he can amend it, reject it, present it as a preparatory exercise, qualify it, complement it, change it. However, even he cannot completely free himself from the words in which he has expressed his thoughts. A complete denial of his past would break him. Yet he is not inexorably bound to it — as his text would be if it did not receive assistance from others or himself. The speaker is not an object that can be analyzed from all directions in order to discover its structure, significance, and presuppositions. He is wholly absorbed in addressing his listeners; he can be listened to, but he cannot be objectified. One can admire his words or conclude that he has nothing to say. But, never is he an object that one can choose or refuse to study. A philosopher puts his listeners in a dilemma: to turn towards or away from him. Between condemnation, contempt, and the refusal to listen on the one hand, and listening or replying, contesting or agreeing with what he says on the other, it is not possible to assume an "objective" attitude in which the speaker is nothing more than a spoken text. The subjectivity of the speaker forces me to have a "subjective" reaction of rejection, indifference, or participation in his thinking: an answer to his presence. Neither one of us can escape the necessity of justifying ourselves to each other. Right from the beginning, speaking creates a double responsibility: the listener cannot refuse to respond to the thinker who is justifying his thoughts to him, and a refusal to listen is an explicit aversion that requires its own justification.

2. Learning

The individual effort that philosophical instruction evokes is the practice of independent thinking. Facts and authoritative statements are unimportant. What is offered wants to be absorbed by an insight that can justify itself. Absorbing is merely a beginning: a preparation for the development of one's own thinking, for which one must accept the responsibility. The function of instruction is to show weak points, ambiguites, mistakes and to stimulate thinking by exemplary arguments and questions. Pupils must discover better ways of thinking. Instruction is always self-instruction. Teachers are useful if they encourage self-criticism.

Does the learning process end with the attainment of a completely independent and accomplished thinking? Is a "master philosopher" autarchic? If this were true, the ideal of doing philosophy would be a self-justifying monologue that ignored anyone else. In confronting other philosophers, an accomplished philosopher would learn, in this case, nothing new. Such a monologue might still be useful as a means of rewarding one's philosophical triumph. While curiosity would remain possible for a philosopher who had "arrived," the philosophical past would no longer be of any interest to him.

If a monologue were the final goal of self-instruction in philosophy, the accomplished philosopher would step beyond the concert of philosophers to unfold his truth alone. Conversations would only be meaningful as long as he had something to communicate. Whoever disagreed would be considered a potential pupil. His speech would be a kind of generosity or vanity; "communicativeness" would not be a matter of necessity.

A period of monologue is not necessarily a *nunc stans*, or an eternity. For if philosophical activity were possible in total isolation, it would still remain a kind of learning process insofar as the experience of thinking in this isolation would go on via aporias and impasses, searching for breakthroughs, evaluating itself, making leaps, discovering new perspectives, and experimenting with original hypotheses. Egology implies a "conversation of the soul with itself."[9] The experience of the thinking consciousness — even in the all-encompassing conception of Hegel — is an entire history of half- and whole discoveries, reversals, transformations, and distortions. In this sense, philosophizing is always learning something new "in addition to . . . ," unless a philosopher is so petrified that he just endlessly repeats himself.

Is a philosophy that is so turned back into itself, its entire history taking place within the framework of one "soul," possible? Not only does it seem possible, but if appearances are not deceiving, it has actually happened in the history of Western philosophy. It is of course difficult to find examples of thinkers who had absolutely no points of contact with other thinkers — at the least their language and problems were related to those of others. But most Western philosophers stood as confident individuals who thought themselves exclusively responsible for the statements they made and the insights they developed. When a philosopher quoted another, he did so to cite problems, to evaluate and amend given solutions, but not because he felt himself to be only one of many participants in a collective search for the truth. The others existed for him as possible contributors to his insight. He alone was the supreme judge. Some spoke of higher judges: God, the Spirit, History, but they initiated themselves into the secrets of the Most High and eventually attained an absolute knowledge of their own.

While Plato and some other philosophers wrote dialogues, these dialogues were in fact veiled monologues wherein the writer created a partner out of his own doubts and contradictions. To state it somewhat exaggeratedly: Western philosophy has been a series of monologues connected to one another by familiar problems and solutions. Although a similar "spirit" holds them together, conversation is not explicitly accepted as the foundation of thinking.

Is this not one of the reasons why something essential is lacking in Western philosophy? Not only is its egological character accompanied by a very poor practice and theory of dialogue but it also suffers from an inability to formulate the individual as such philosophically. Does this not reveal a profound lack of self-awareness on the part of the thinking subject? Is monology the illness of our culture?

It is by no means the intention of this book to play into the hands of dialogical and "democratic" glorifiers of talking — of talking through and talking out — who, in flight from their own and others' inferiority, seek the solution to everything in an endless series of clichés, slogans, and common adages. Very few conversations enrich the interlocutors' insight. No conversation is fruitful unless the participants carry on the critical conversation further *with themselves*, long splendidly practiced and analyzed by the Western philosophical and religious traditions. The apology given in this book for the radical necessity of philosophical conversation is as much against the superficiality of conversation techniques and theories, which only produce idle talk, as it is against the more profound forgetting of concrete philosophical starting points, which can never be overcome.

The starting point and abiding basis of philosophy is not to be found in a thinking ego alone but rather in a principally unlimited discussion. Through discussion a multitude of fundamentally different viewpoints interact with one another, such that a relationship and solidarity among them is uncovered, yet is established in a way that does not allow their truth to be summarized in a new and final monologue. If this thesis is correct, there is something wrong with every monological philosophy. Conversation, then, is more than a practical, psychological, or sociohistorical inevitability. It belongs to the essence and foundation of philosophy itself. Philosophy is, fundamentally and necessarily, an intersubjective reality.

3. Discussion with existing philosophies

If the essence of philosophy implies discussion and intersubjectivity, a philosopher can never announce the final truth *ex cathedra* but will always remain dependent on listening and learning. In relation to other philosophies, every philosopher remains a pupil. Before one enters into a discussion with them, one must plunge into the contexts and constellations of their thoughts. A philosopher can learn the most from those superior to him. The study of the greatest works takes an enormous amount of time. But, understanding less profound colleagues demands a great deal of time and effort as well. The attempt to understand other philosophies frequently fails. As pointed out earlier, most of the great philosophers were too engrossed in their own approaches and thoughts to do justice, in their criticism, to other philosophers. They did not fully benefit from the fecundation offered by others. Can the monological structure of Western philosophy be attributed to the cultural discouragement of participation by women thinkers at the very highest levels? Does the sterility of Western individualism come from its "homosexuality"?

The philosophies from which one allows one's own thinking to be fed, shocked, criticized, supplemented, or amended are a pregiven and forethought reality and, in that sense, are a philosophical *past*. This past exists in the form of spoken words and written texts. A philosopher learns most from — and yet seldom has the chance to speak to — the greatest thinkers, which are few in every era. Hence, written texts are especially important. But, even the word that one contemporary thinker directs to another can be considered as a forethought and immediate past. In this sense there is no principal difference between words just spoken, published works of "contemporaries" written yesterday or thirty years ago, and the old texts of classical philosophers.

Does the history of philosophy, then, include any philosophy that has been pronounced? What is left for thematic philosophy? Does this only exist in the present and future of a thinker who here and now thinks further about what has been thought by others and by himself? In this case, all thematic philosophy would be a participation in the history of philosophy, and all introductions would be historical. All orientation and acquaintance, explanation and commentary would then belong to the one all-encompassing historical practice of philosophy, and the construction of a system would be nothing more than a specific kind of continuation of remote or recent pasts.

Each act of speaking or writing transforms thoughts into a presence that immediately becomes history. The question arises, then, whether there really is a difference between a philosophy spoken yesterday and one written 2,500 years ago. The works a philosopher turns to, with the desire to learn and receive inspiration, must be of high quality — that is, they must help the reader acquire truths and insights in a philosophical way. When they were written is not an essential consideration. Or, so one might think. However, are truth and insight independent of the time in which they are pronounced? Can one dissociate truth from the language, from its references, resonances, and all the cultural presuppositions through which it is revealed in any philosophy? Is philosophical truth eternal, in the sense that it can remain identical and merely change costumes as the times change? The question, what parts of the philosophical past are important for contemporary systematics, goes back to the problem of the relation between truth and time, which is the constant context of the thoughts formulated here. The question of which authors one should turn to can be approached by reflecting on the difference between what is "classical" and what is "contemporary."

4. "Classical" and "contemporary"

According to one conception, it is possible to understand every philosophy as an atemporal, or supertemporal, core set in time-, place-, and culture-bound forms. It can be freed from these forms by a translation, or interpretation, that transfers this core to another time, place, and culture. The essence of a philosophy will then be independent of its outer trappings. Whatever the merits of this conception may be, it is important to realize that no concrete philosophy can be presented in a form beyond all time. This has indeed been tried, for example by certain Thomist and Marxist schools, who attempted a repetition and literal translation of their masters' thoughts. These attempts, however, are doomed to fail, because every presentation is itself necessarily a moment of a particular culture — and no culture exists externally. A "literal" translation of the *Summa* into twentieth-century English, for example, changes its *entire* meaning; one cannot avoid this by adding notes and commentaries explaining the difference in the meanings of 'substance', 'accident', 'matter' and 'nature' in the thirteenth century and today. When a text comes from a culture that is fundamentally different from ours, a translation is only meaningful as a reference to the original and as a first commentary. This is why extensive clarifications of the text are indispensable and more fitting than simple translations of old texts into "modern" English (simultaneously involving a form of "modern" thinking). Translations of old texts without commentary cry out for an interpreter who can point to meanings that are veiled within the text.

Translations, as well as elaborations, by epigones — their applications, paraphrases, and repetitions — change and enervate the great philosophies of our past. Many neo-Thomistic, neo-Kantian, neo-Hegelian, and neo-Marxist attempts to understand reality are brought stillborn to the world. They can be useful as introductions to and explanations of the understanding of Thomas, Kant, Hegel, and Marx. But if they do not make themselves superfluous, by encouraging a study of their sources, they miss their mark. In their impotent attempts at retaining an old core in modern packaging, they are old-fashioned and provoke our aversion. Even now the originals speak better and more strongly than their updated shadows and extractions. And yet, they are still not voices of our time. Masterpieces ask for transformations, not repetitions. Loyalty to the great thinkers of the past means that we must leave them behind as we think further. For we can only be genuine in our own way. Mindless repetition of great thoughts is treason; a certain kind of opposition — thinking differently — is a necessity. However, not every rebellion is genuine, and not every opposition is thinking.

Another kind of repetition is possible. I will use the word *retaking* for it. Plotinus's reprise of Plato, or Hegel's *"Aufhebung"* of Aristotle, were not exercises in archaism but were rather (re)creations far superior to most of the works of their more "original" contemporaries. The renewals accomplished by the great philosophers were partly due to their assimilation of preceding thoughts. Within the new context of their own times, cultures, and psyches, they recollected the fruits of old thoughts, which only seemed worn out. A new thinker is just as much a father as he is a son of his father.

To understand the process of creative reproduction, the recognition of the difference between core and outer trappings is insufficient. Only a thorough transformation of this core can bring a dead thought back to life. A thinker not only appropriates (a part of) his own past but, through his remembrance, produces a new kind of life for an earlier thought. Thanks to a new fecundity, it has not really passed away.

How are old and new related in the life of philosophy? What do 'living,' 'dying,' 'being dead,' 'reviving,' 'being born,' 'growing,' 'developing' mean here? Is this kind of metaphorical imagery sufficient to show the ways of moving, proceeding, retreating, deepening, and levelling peculiar to philosophy? Is it an improvement when we replace organic metaphors with mechanical, geometrical, or algebraic ones?

The question that arose in the course of this chapter was less comprehensive, although in itself difficult enough: it seems that philosophy and independent thinking, here and now, can be characterized as an activity "of our time," as something contemporary. If doing philosophy always implies learning, the great thinkers of our past — who have produced the acknowledged "classics" of thought — have a special and indispensable significance for the continuation of independent thought. In this way, the question concerning the relation between thematic philosophy and philosophical history takes the form of a question concerning the relation between what is "classic" and what is "contemporary".

What do we mean by "our time" and "contemporary"? The time in which we live and think cannot be clearly distinguished from a time said to be past. Our time is full of echoes from earlier ages; our culture lives out of many and various inheritances, which form its capital and its resources. We are filled with the past: our culture does not form a unity in itself. "We" are a collection of groups, individuals, and tendencies that are profoundly different from one another. It is difficult to recognize a common denomination in our feelings, thoughts, and actions. "Our time" and "our culture" do not refer to one permanent source of capital from which we can all draw. The present heritage, for example, in the form of available literature (not necessarily read), lessons (not necessarily listened to), libraries (not necessarily used), sayings (not necessarily understood), and ideologies (not necessarily demystified), must first be appropriated before it can play a role in defining our time. Many possibilities for revival remain unused; much dead material is forgotten or destroyed anew. The parts of our past that will bloom again depend on the attention they receive from various persons and groups, here and now. For some of our contemporaries the Bible is more present than the work of Newton and Euclid. For others it is the other way around. In spite of the century separating us from Marx, he is for many a very relevant guide. Heidegger's work, on the other hand, is considered by some archaic. "Our time" is a collective name for a great diversity of ways in which groups and individuals — during a certain imprecisely circumscribed time (the seventies, the period after 1945, after 1918, after 1900) — have acquired and transformed parts of "our" traditions. Receptivity, along with selection, discovery, and (re)creation are essential moments in the constitution of the culture and the cultures that characterize a certain period. "Our time" involves the originality of timely choices and transformations, through which genuine transmitters of culture recognize and, in their self-willed way, act on the possibilities they encounter. Their self-will gives a new twist to current styles and conceptions, which are renewed in such a way that they inaugurate a new time.

    In addition to the renewing and surprising element resisting a mere synchronic study of culture and time, the traditions and high points acknowledged today are so varied that a global characterization of the "values and norms of our time" is very difficult. Perhaps we cannot go any further than to sketch some of the formal aspects, such as the mausoleality mentioned above, with its related pluralism, relativism, and primitivism, and their consequent impasses. However, everyone can find a few allies and models from the many offered in history and can keep these as companions for life. This is the only way to participate in our culture. Those who do this form a concert, in which all possible tones and harmonies can be heard; they share parts and perspectives of their history and call it "our heritage" or "the past."

If "the philosophy of our time" includes an available heritage as well as a multitude of selective assimilations, chronological simultaneity is not enough for unanimity with regard to fundamental problems. This also explains why some feel a greater affinity with Plato or Aristotle than with some of our famous or talented contemporaries. Philosophical proximity or distance are not directly proportional to the shortness or length of the chronological time separating us from our predecessors. Simultaneity admits of distance and strangeness. Temporal gaps are bridged by a reflective association with the past that also "re-presents" it in order to prepare for a future.

Does this mean, then, that "contemporaneity" cannot be a criterion for judging the quality of a philosophy? Even if it cannot be, two aspects of good philosophy still plead for the necessity of its contemporary character: comprehensibility and genuineness.

Philosophy must be *comprehensible*, here and now. This does *not* mean that it must be understandable to everyone or that it must associate itself with common ideas, language, and slogans in vogue. A philosopher writes primarily for those who already have a fairly high level of understanding. They rightly expect philosophy, as a part of spiritual life, to speak the language of this life as it is lived "here and now." This is not only necessary in terms of comprehensibility, but a philosophy will also not be *genuine* if a thinker has left his own time with its current schemas, associations, and languages to settle in a bygone past or in an unknown future. As a participant in the life of a specific epoch, one cannot pretend to live outside the customs and idiosyncrasies, associations and manners of one's contemporaries. Every philosophy necessarily bears the traces of a certain solidarity, even if it has a very original or exceptional character brought about by the inner distance that accompanies the most thorough reflection. Someone who truly reflects on genuine problems is very concrete; a great thinker is distinguished by his extreme sensitivity to the prevailing situation — enabling him to discover the historical roots and background of the "here and now" and the seeds of tomorrow — and his ability to go beyond the superficial meaning of current events.

Genuineness distinguishes true philosophy from old-fashioned and fashionable rhetoric, futuristic projections of present superficialities, exoticisms, and esoteric vogues. It is, however, not enough. Philosophy must also bring one closer to the *truth* — or bring the truth closer. Real demons or real scoundrels are genuinely what they are, but they are not examples to be imitated. The popular opinions, methods, and fashions of our time distort and pervert the truth. A good philosophy is therefore necessarily "untimely." Even those who can no longer believe in the possibility of approaching "the truth," or any truth, must take this unadaptedness to "the time" into account. Little would be left to philosophy if it gave up all critical distance from the commonplaces of its time. Sailing on the waves of fashionable chatter has little to do with philosophy, even when such sailing is brought into logically perfect form and clarity.

The "untimeliness" of philosophy can be masked by a return to the past. Despite the archaic impression some philosophies give at first sight, they may be much nearer to the truth than the attractive novelties substantiating the current fame and influence of many internationally acclaimed philosophers. The true and genuine character of solid philosophy exists in the new possibilities it offers to an industrious and thoughtful reader, who seeks to understand what true reality is and why it is so. On this level — a level that cannot be dissociated from its interpretation in time-bound images, thoughts, tendencies, events, and expressions — the issue of old and new is unimportant, unless one means "new" precisely as something to learn from studying a (recent, older, or ancient) philosophy.

Nevertheless, it seems plausible to consider contemporary philosophy ahead of past philosophies, in view of our wide historical knowledge — as to which solutions succeeded or failed. This impression presupposes, however, that (1) we can determine which given solutions were right or wrong; (2) we can truly experience and thoroughly understand the content of past philosophies; and (3) the history of philosophy can be understood as a series of answers to problems that do not change radically but remain the same, or form immutable parts of new problems. These three presuppositions form an implicit theory of the history of philosophy that is not readily evident. In the following chapters, various aspects of this theory will be discussed. For the time being, the following considerations of the problem of contemporaneity will suffice.

For this reason alone, what comes later is not better. Something ancient is often wiser than the *dernier cri*. Is the element of time useful in determining the quality and the (relative) truth of a present or past philosophy? The only criterion is in the truth attained or approached in a successful way. The only way to apply this standard is through a new thinking that, here and now, reproduces the truth differently. If the "rethinking" of a former thought favors the formation of correct thoughts, or if an older thought allows the development of correct thoughts more quickly and easily, thinking from the past deserves recognition: it is a good pacesetter for contemporary thought.

It is possible, however, for one to recognize the quality of a former philosophy without understanding its entire breadth and depth. One may understand it well enough to have a general idea of its strength and to give due credit to its uncomprehended aspects. It is not necessary for a good music critic to be a great composer or musician; in philosophy, too, it is possible to be an authority without being an original thinker.

The idea of a new philosophy's having a greater chance of being true than an earlier one is irresistible when one takes the history of sciences like physics and chemistry as a model for the history of thought. The abandonment of certain conceptions to make way for a new consensus seems at least partially attributable to the strength of certain arguments and the evidence of tried (hypo)theses. The works of earlier scientists and the textual reports on their efforts fulfill a liberating and therapeutic role in the expansion of our insights. In a shorter period of time we can come as far as our predecessors did. A crisis sometimes arises in a discipline, shaking the whole edifice to its foundations. After a victory over such a crisis, however, a great deal of formerly acquired knowledge is still saved from the ruins.

The foundations of philosophy can neither be compared to definitely established theses or hypotheses nor to provisional fundamentals that, through a continuous process of amendment and correction, attain greater precision and are insured against mistakes. Since philosophy is an attempt to understand things thoroughly, it does not aim at derived theses, hypotheses, and theories but rather at insights into grounds that make thinking, establishing, experiencing, guessing, searching, and reasoning possible. Until starting points are transparent and clear, philosophy cannot rest. But is this goal attainable? Should we not suspect the "attainability" of clear and certain answers to most fundamental questions? If this suspicion is correct, the history of philosophy consists in a continuous starting over, trying, seeking, and daring; it will be an unceasing experimentation with starting points and opinions that must eventually show what can be discovered and understood. The essential radicalism of philosophy involves the impossibility of simply abolishing earlier attempts and procceding from a higher level that we assume has been attained. A philosopher is an eternal beginner, and therefore an apprentice to everyone who has made the same attempt before him. As he goes on, he develops a relationship with the other diggers and builders, who are irreplaceable as the creators of the classics of philosophy. The quality of a philosophical work has little to do with the point in time in which it is written. The history of thought may be compared to a court of justice, but it is surely not the supreme judge itself. Philosophies can only be judged by a profound thinking that cuts across time and forms a kinship with profound thinkers of the past.

The meaning of earlier philosophies depends on what our own thought can do with them. What this meaning is cannot be defined by ascertaining a portion of the truth contained in an earlier philosophy. It does not contain any truth unless some living thinker (re)thinks it. Its importance depends on the correctness with which a thinker reproduces the possible truth in this earlier philosophy. Much experience, imagination, strength of thought, and affinity is needed to lay open the truth in an existing work. The value of historical philosophies can only be measured by a thinker who, here and now, tries and tests them in order to establish their solidity. Only he can form a judgment — against which the "history of thought" is powerless.

Independent thinking is the task. But does it not destroy the meaningfulness of all historical viewpoints?

5. To which philosophers must I turn?

If philosophy is always a learning process (see Sections 2 and 3), the matter of choosing teachers and texts is itself an essential moment of philosophy. If the history of philosophy can be understood as an exploration and presentation of the texts of the great teachers of our past, it is necessarily an element of thematic philosophy. Of course, no philosopher can familiarize himself with all the philosophies of the past. Even a philosophical historian cannot achieve such completeness; neither can it be delegated to research. Then who knows and rethinks history as a whole?

Philosophers think as individuals, on their own. I cannot contract for others to do my own thinking. A teacher can help me to find the right way, analyze a philosophical work, learn how others pose and solve certain questions, check or develop a rational argument, suggest viewpoints, and so on. But I must redo all this preparatory work. Thoughts dissolve if they are not animated and preserved by a living (re)thinking. Ideas cannot be displayed as can lifeless minerals and stuffed birds; they only exist in the form of actual acts of thought.

A philosopher or historian who can absorb *all* the thoughts of the past is not possible, if for no other reason than that he does not have enough time to do so. But is completeness a philosophical ideal? How are historical completeness and truth related? Identifying the truth with "the whole," in an historical sense, presupposes that all philosophies contain a certain element of truth and that they are all necessary in composing the whole truth, which can only be achieved after the history of the philosophical search for truth is completed. No philosophy can be completely wrong or superfluous. In this view, the history of philosophy is inspired by a power that attains its goal by means of war and harmony: the many perspectives and foundations that acquire power on the level of philosophy join together under an omniscient eye as one whole.

Such a conception of truth, philosophy, and history can be characterized as an interesting form of teleological and synthetical thinking. It cannot realize its pretensions *in concreto* unless it identifies completeness and quality with a self-made selection from the history of philosophy. Because it joins truth with totality, it must maintain that such a selection is sufficient to confirm its concept of philosophy and history. This thesis would be right if philosophical life at various times could be reduced to a few principle types, expressing what is essential in each period, and if each of these principal types could be viewed as variations on one theme, which would appear to full advantage in the last, all-inclusive symphony closing the history of philosophy.

How can one prove all of these presuppositions? For the time being it is more realistic to proceed from the irrefutable fact that human beings do not have enough time or energy to put themselves into the thought worlds of more than ten philosophers. Then, since life is short and preparation for genuine philosophy is long, which philosophies must one study, not only as pleasant brain teasers but also for existential interest? It takes years of study and reflection to be comfortable in the philosophy of Spinoza or Kant or Aristotle. Is the price not too high for the lessons they will give? A person cannot answer this question before studying these thinkers. What arguments can make him accept the risk of disappointment?

The quality of a philosophical text or teacher cannot be determined externally. Within the realm of philosophy, the only authority is one's own thinking. Someone can be a good professional critic without being an original thinker, but he cannot manage without his own powers of reflection and consideration.

A beginner does not yet have sufficient knowledge of philosophy to make a solid judgment about the teachers and texts he needs. He therefore is dependent on the *authority* of others, whose reliability can only be determined through a belief in further authorities. One can choose to rely on great names, on numerous publications, on opinions of the media, on advice from family, friends, and acquaintances, or even on the desire to defy authority. Fashion can also be influential in the study of philosophy. Even some famous "philosophers" succumb to the popular voices of the day. Perhaps this explains their fame for a certain period of time.

Initially, a student depends on the authority of his teachers. But his teachers are chosen or recommended by others. What are the qualifications of these others? What criteria do they use? Who judges if the criteria are applied correctly? And so on. Questioning the competence of critics and the correctness of their conclusions results in an endless regression, unless one knows an acceptable and indisputable authority. Unfortunately, such an authority does not exist.

Neither the number nor the power of those who shout the loudest carries any weight before the forum of reason. This forum is neither a collection of all the professors of philosophy nor the sum of all those who publish the most; nor is it the most popular or well-paid group of speakers in current lecture circuits. Only a genuine philosopher can judge the quality of available philosophies. Only one who genuinely questions and knows has any authority to judge the quality of professors, publishers, and debaters claiming state-of-the-art knowledge in philosophy.

A beginner cannot rely on the standards that are supposed to distinguish philosophers. Some teachers are more "open," "inspiring," scholarly, intelligent, sharp, clear, and revealing than others. However important all these may be, however intimate the relation they maintain to good philosophy, they still do not necessarily make good philosophers.[10]

If none of the authorities to whom a pupil can appeal are reliable, the situation seems hopeless. But can we not assume the possibility of immediate recognition of genuine philosophical thinking? Perhaps some people have a better feel for it than others. Since philosophy has its roots in the core of being human, the thought that everyone somehow "knows" what philosophy is and can distinguish the genuine from the phony seems unavoidable. However, such a "remembering," through which this "knowledge" is awakened, needs help in being brought to birth.

Is our "preknowledge" enough to recognize good philosophical midwives? Coincidence, and some luck, play a role. But during the learning process, the ability to distinguish good and bad philosophy also develops. When repetition, imitation, appropriation, and practice have led to the development of a pupil's own independent thinking, his critical awareness will also have grown to the point where he can judge his teachers.

A good teacher not only thinks before and for his students, he also does everything he can to help them come to their own critical and productive ways of thinking. He elicits their criticisms, even if he is unable to come out of it unscathed. He welcomes this sort of undoing, if it means that his students are thinking. Of course, criticism from students can be unjust — for instance when they praise "progressive," but superficial, teachers at the cost of solid and apparently old-fashioned instructors who emphasize the formative value of classical texts. It can be a credit, as well as a discredit, to a teacher when he is celebrated. Negative criticisms, worn-out ideas in the guise of modern or "progressive" remarks, or easily comprehensible fads make great and lasting impressions on many adolescents. But even bad or faddish teachers can sometimes spur their students to real thinking. In spite of the erroneous or misleading information generated by their examples, their students sometimes develop enough strength to see the errors, the superficialities, and deficiencies. In forming a school one raises one's pupils to the freedom of autonomous thinking. A pupil who swears by one or more philosophers is a slave, even if the coryphaei on whom he leans are the most critical and emancipated imaginable.

These assertions are not meant to induce unbridled doubt, scepticism, and negative criticism. The inner distance necessary for all masters must be accompanied by a careful treatment of the presented texts. A good teacher knows his responsibility in the choice of these texts: they should preserve the best of our traditions and offer the greatest opportunities for fruitful thinking, which eventually leaves them behind as it makes its way here and now. If the word *truth* still has meaning, and if there are indeed truths to discover, the responsibility of a teacher involves not only a pupil's training in the formal aspects of thinking but also his acquisition of true and probable ideas. If philosophy were no longer a search for truth or wisdom, every nonformal difference between teachers and students, advanced and beginning philosophers, reasonable and foolish people, philosophers and babies would disappear. Although one person might think more clearly or have greater synthetic faculty than another, no one would have to bother discovering what can be justifiably claimed or stated, as far as the content of ideas is concerned. Everyone would be as wise as the next person. One would merely watch out for gibberish, and contradictions would have to be avoided. But one might ask, why. If it were no longer a question of truth, thinking would suppress the earnest passion of seeking. Philosophy would be degraded to a pleasant pastime divorced from "real life." There would be no such words as *meaningful* and *meaningless.* In one's growing up and development, no ideals or "values" could be recommended, for nothing would make any difference. Childish opinions would have the same status as those of the "sages." Pedagogy, like our museums, would be a mere presentation of all the possible alternatives and techniques for discovering what one wants. In philosophy, everyone would merely have to decide what he wanted to think. A preference for certain texts could no longer be justified. Only formal-logical qualities could function as criteria, unless one also regarded clarity and coherence as unnecessary features of knowledge. If every baby were just as wise as Plato, there would no longer be a place for philosophy. The history of philosophy would merely contain curiosities, pieces of interesting information, and symptoms of a peculiar tendency to concoct difficult thoughts. This history would not be interesting since it could not be continued.

However, if truth is still possible and philosophy may remain a passion, a scholar of philosophy cannot escape the question standing before all beginners: to which masters shall I turn? Which texts must I read?

Taking a book in hand always entails the giving of a certain credit. Even an accomplished philosopher (if such a thing is possible) cannot say with certainty whether the text he is going to read is good or not. He, too, is dependent on authorities: colleagues, quotations and references in texts he has read, recommendations by the media, publishers, and professional associations. Of course, philosophical exercises refine one's taste and judgment, but one's preferences reflect just as much on oneself as on valued or rejected authors.

The decision to study a certain philosophy depends on a judgment concerning not only its intrinsic value, but also its ability to mean something, here and now, for the person who studies it. One can recognize the greatness of some philosophers without being drawn to spend much time on them. Some texts lie beyond my intellectual horizon (which does not have to be and cannot be all-inclusive); others deal with subjects that seem confused and superficial; others strike me as strange.

But perhaps those strange texts are precisely the ones I need! It can be pleasant and fruitful to deal with familiar authors; however, a certain alienation is necessary to avoid short-sightedness and obsession with so-called self-evident truths. Both relationship and strangeness are necessary, and yet each demands a particular approach. The greedy openness of an octopus narrows and kills. The desire to absorb everything leads to a pedantic, petty housing for the greatest thinking in the tiny lodging of one's brain. The right kind of openness is also different from totalization and synthesis. It is rather like a grand tour: temporarily escaping from the familiarity of a home becoming increasingly opaque; cautiously exposing oneself to other climates with different presuppositions and experiments. I must learn to *think otherwise* "to come to myself" in a new, different, and more seasoned way. The assistance of thinkers who dispute my foundations and limitations is necessary to overcome my old thoughts. I need good enemies to lead the fight for more truth.

In my search for good guidance, chance and good luck come into play. Not all texts are available, and those that are demand time before I can know if I must read them at all. The Western democratization of culture has led (thank goodness!) to a flood of good editions, but much time is lost in working through useless or overly lengthy works. Once we have found a proper way of thinking, we must leave many unread. Discrimination, a careful cultivation of relationships, and a passion for battling with great opponents and good strangers are strongly needed, in order to know which philosophies have to be studied.

Pupils as well as teachers change preferences, relationships, and favorite enemies as they proceed. In different times, in different phases of problematics and reflection, *other* others are necessary. A thinker's choice of texts and partners for discussion has a history. Thinking is a production that obeys an inner urgency and a specific regularity. Choice and interiority are, however, not the sole determinants. Like every history, the history of thought, too, is determined to a certain degree by coincidences and influences arising not from the thinking individual, but from external circumstances: colleagues who attack him, reviews that misunderstand or excoriate his works, students he cannot convince, or texts that he reads by chance.

A genuine philosopher cannot be a plaything of history because he is actively present and involved in it; he wants to measure himself against thoughts that may be surprising or strange. Although he does not pretend to have an all-inclusive viewpoint, his participation in the history of thought lies in an original way of assimilating a selection of the utterances that struck his mind. As a history of information, instruction, and training, the history of philosophy is essentially incomplete.

6. Consequences for a history of philosophy

Philosophizing is a unity of appropriation and alienation. We must go outside ourselves and enter into other thoughts, but we must also transform them into our own. This process, however, does not constitute a dialectical synthesis whereby everything else is assimilated into the identity of one main philosopher. Rather, it creates a unity wherein the otherness of different thinkers is recognized and preserved in a specific way, which has yet to be determined. The relation of the Other and the Same is not a fusion.

From the structure of philosophical research as described in the previous sections, a number of consequences follow for the history of philosophy. If a historical account of philosophical thought is motivated by a desire to continue the past and the present life of philosophy, it will necessarily bear the characteristics of this discipline, which is an essential element of independent thinking.

6.1 Why "the history of philosophy" cannot be written

An immediate consequence is that the history of philosophy cannot be written. If I try to write it without help, I am forced, on physical grounds alone, to base most of my work on secondary literature. In addition to various pragmatic limitations, I cannot escape the fact that my selection of movements, authors, and texts as well as my rendition of relevant questions, ideas, argumentations, schemes, and systems betray my explicit or implicit personal philosophy. If I am not aware of this — for example, by uncritically following a trend — I will believe and claim my story to be the story of philosophy, when in fact it is merely a rendition of how this history looks from my particular viewpoint.

Every historical overview of philosophy expresses a particular thematic philosophy that functions as a prism, through which the philosophical light radiated into our history is refracted. The selection and interpretation of the philosophers discussed are expressions of another philosophy: the philosophy of the historian, who plays the role of stage manager. At worst his tale teaches only what he holds to be true. The history of philosophy will, then, appear as a series of attempts at formulating the "true" philosophy of the historian. When all truth can be summarized in one last, all-inclusive synthesis, the history of philosophy will lose its importance. It can still

be useful from a didactic viewpoint, but it will no longer be an essential movement of thought. The same can be said, however, of a
history of philosophy that does not strive for a synthesis but allows
itself a final judgment on the good and evil in philosophy, elevating
Ockhamistic razors and personal standards to the level of the highest
criteria and playing the supreme judge.

A history written by an author who keeps himself in the
background and strives for neutrality might seem freer from prejudice and may appear more instructive. But neutrality is not possible. Selection itself demands that choice, on the basis of insight or
assumption regarding the importance of the material involved, be
made. A rendition of the content and structure of a certain
philosophy demands a thinking that is at least sympathetic to its line
of thought. If its problems and struggles are not recognized, this
philosophy is not worth mentioning. In fact, "neutrality" always con-
ceals a particular philosophy. In its selection and discussions a
"neutral" philosophy normally follows the "usual" list of names and
divisions consecrated by a particular tradition. A hallowed series of
authors, schools, problems, and discussions appears again and
again, without any critical stance towards the source of all those
schemas and hidden evaluations. Such a view is itself the product of
a traditional look at philosophy and its history. A *genuine* history of
philosophy *and of its history* must discover how philosophy and traditional philosophical history both came to be, who made the traditional selections and divisions of authors, texts, and topics, why certain names are not included in certain periods, and so forth. A good
history of philosophy justifies its own presuppositions and criteria; it
is simultaneously a philosophical illumination of other histories of
philosophy and an explanation of its own implicit philosophy.

Many problems present themselves here. First of all: Who
decides who the greatest specialists are? Must the decision maker not
at least be highly knowledgeable on the matter in question? Who
decides who is knowledgeable? The fact that someone has written a
great deal on Plato or has read his works for years does not
automatically make him a good interpreter. If one relies on the
names frequently mentioned at conventions or in publications, one
depends on the authority of those mentioning the names. But, do
they really have the capacity to judge? The organizer of a team
effort — the editor of an encyclopedia, for example — must decide

who should write a particular section. His decision mirrors his knowledge of each subject and his trust in his advisors. He must also decide which parts of the history, which philosophers, problems, texts, and schools must be discussed, how they must be presented, (in what order and length), and so on. These decisions presuppose a certain vision of the history as a whole, the importance and significance of various philosophers and their interrelation, the meaning of the problems discussed, and so on. It presupposes an insight into the history of philosophy. This insight will be illustrated and confirmed in the execution of the proposed plan. However, the question as to its correctness can only be answered after all other possible plans have been compared to it. As long as this is not done — and this is not physically possible — every encyclopedia and all other histories are only expressions of a particular and limited perspective of philosophy and its history.

You could, of course, decide to treat *all* authors and schools considered to be important by professional philosophers, but you cannot escape the necessity of designating places and functions to these true, or so-called, philosophers and the roles they play in this history. However, in so doing, you make a decision as to their relevance. The value judgments underlying this decision are once again expressions of your philosophy.

Arranging philosophers according to birth dates is not the solution either. Such a gallery of separate figures will not constitute a history and cannot be read without previous knowledge of the names of this historical *who's who*. Consistency, and the avoidance of any semblance of value judgments, will mean devoting an equal amount of space to every name. Such a levelling, however, is just what philosophical thinking is not.

A third problem arises when several historians of philosophy collaborate. Their personal philosophies do not necessarily coincide. For example, an Aristotelian scholar may personally be an idealist, while an excellent Kantian scholar may be empirically oriented. In order to guarantee unity in the work, the editor of an encyclopedia will usually look for collaborators with similar thinking. In doing so, the editor accepts that the discussion will have a limited perspective. The spiritual climate of the resulting work depends to a great extent on the openness of the collaborators' perspective. The editor might also entrust each section to the specialist with the greatest affinity for that particular subject. As a result, this collective production would contain greatly differing treatments, as each specialist revived the spirit of his subject. Such a book would reflect an image of the constantly diverging positions in philosophy. But here, too, the problems discussed above will surface: (1) who should organize the battle between philosophies and their interpreters? and (2) who should decide who the suitable and spiritually compatible exegetes of the philosophies are? These questions become more pressing in connection with the great and many-sided philosophies such as those of Plato, Aquinas, Hegel, Nietzsche, Levinas, and others. Whose thought can grasp these great philosophers? To understand them thoroughly, one must perhaps be a great philosopher oneself. But then one runs the risk of absorbing philosophies into one's own original, new philosophy.

We need not spend much time on histories imposed by ideologies and institutionalized religions as their official documentation of the past. The power trying to legitimize itself through such apparent genealogies would appear ridiculous if it were not so deadly. Within genuine spiritual life, too, the endless demagogic repetition of the same slander robs us of a genuine past, and thus of the capacity to profit from its greatest works. The ideological terror of a political or (quasi-)religious concentration of power results in an even greater primitivism and barbarism than does the dictatorship of common sense, reigning over and ruling a "free society."

6.2 *Every history of philosophy is an expression of a thematic philosophy*

Every history of philosophy implies a particular philosophical perspective. Thus, there are just as many histories of philosophy as there are philosophers. Considering that, based on their similarity, certain philosophers can be grouped together, we can simplify this fact (and make it cruder) by speaking of types of philosophy and of philosophical history. Traditional labels such as 'positivism', 'idealism', 'rationalism', 'logical empiricism', and so forth are attempts at a typology that is also applicable to the history of philosophy.

To avoid naiveté, the author of philosophical history must be aware of his presuppositions and perspectives. The same is true of the reader who — to evaluate such a history properly — must discover its explicit or implicit philosophy. Author and reader must both undertake a thematic philosophizing, if they are not to be swept uncritically away by their own or others' opinions. Those who claim neutrality and objectivity in the rendition of the philosophical past are the most naive of all: they lack all reflection and method. Nobody can write a good history of philosophy unless he is a good philosopher. *History is not the hiding place for people who cannot succeed in thematic philosophy.*

A student introduced to philosophy through the study of its history must learn that he encounters an implicit (thematic) thinking, unaccounted for in such a history. This hidden thinking represents an authority of whom he is initially unaware. Learning to do philosophy involves challenging these hidden authorities and urging them to justify themselves. Such reactions are the beginning of one's discussion with the thematic philosophy that dominates each history. The student discovers that he cannot blindly trust any history of philosophy, because a historical introduction presupposes a thematic aspect, and every thematic philosophy presupposes its author's discussion with existing philosophies. Thus, the study of philosophy and its history reveals a specific circularity.

We must give up the illusion of having the entire museum of philosophy's past at our disposal, allowing us to take out and examine at will any artifacts we wish. Our memories are not universal. Our libraries bear the marks of individual and changing preferences. The furnishing of a museum, a library, an overview, a textbook is always an expression of someone's thematic position: his friendships and battles, victories and defeats, suspicions and desires. Every philosophical museum, every "philosophical library," and every encyclopedia is characterized by *individuality*. Every synthesis is based on a particular perspective.

Such an insight makes us modest. Imperialistic claims, presenting individual viewpoints as if they were complete and universal truths, betray a blindness to the arguable assumptions ruling their visions. In writing about our past, a self-aware historian knows that he partakes in the ongoing discussion constituting the actual life of thematic philosophy. All-inclusive syntheses are overextended. Striving for widely inclusive interpretations is not condemned here, for without them philosophy quickly becomes small and petty. Great differences in quality remain possible between a soloist and other members of the orchestra, or between various soloists, but even the most forceful synthesis is also only one part of an entire concert. Neither a Hegelian summary of all the truths ever thought nor a positivistic neutrality is possible. The impartiality deemed to characterize Hegelianism, as well as positivism, is an illusion. While positivism is infinitely more naive than Hegel's account of our history, Hegel himself was not fully aware of the particular preoccupations and unconscious tendencies of his universalistic thought.

6.3 The necessity for a certain "positivism" in the history of philosophy

In spite of the assertions above, a certain positivism, along with a striving for the greatest possible openness and synthesis, is necessary for a serious history of philosophy, since philosophizing always implies learning. This conclusion becomes critical for the following chapter's interpretation of philosophy (thematic as well as historical) as discussion. If the practice of philosophy is not a solipsistic repetition but a speaking and listening so that one may better speak, other philosophies must be allowed the chance to speak *as others*. The other must be heard. A certain reservation is required on my part as listener; putting my own convictions in parentheses, I must be willing to regard my own ideas as a matter for discussion and to take other postulates as possible alternatives. Making the other's position as strong as possible is the best way to escape my own obsessions. To listen is to go on a journey to the grounds and bounds of worlds inhabited by other thinkers. Reading involves following others' trains of thought and entering their labyrinths to explore them from the inside out.

Since great thinkers in our history have treated one another unjustly, listening is an art poorly practiced by creative philosophers. Although they have learned from one another, their renditions of others' thoughts have been distortions, and often caricatures. The incorrect transformations occurring in learning and listening have nonetheless been fruitful: even a half- or poorly understood philosophy seems to inspire great thinkers to great thoughts. Our history might, however, have been more fruitful, more human, and more philosophical if individual philosophers had understood others as others in an exemplary fashion. The many dialogues written since Plato are, as said earlier, disguised monologues — sometimes mere catechetical presentations of a dogmatism trying to subjugate its opponents at any price. We have not progressed very far. Dogmatism, arrogance, neutralism, and easy forms of negativism are in their heyday. Some philosophers only want to hear themselves, or their followers, speak. But even genuine philosophers, concerned with "the thing itself," are sometimes too absorbed in their problems and ideas to give real consideration to other thoughts. A universal openness is probably beyond our capacity. Striving to do others justice, however, remains essential for a true description of philosophy's past and present.

6.4 *Specific problems of the history of philosophy*

What kind of positivism is required for a just history of philosophy? The life of philosophy must be understood and explained "from the inside out." But how?

6.4.1 INDIVIDUAL PHILOSOPHERS

The initial questions in this context are: How should a history of philosophy begin? Who or what "makes" the history of philosophy? Must "philosophical life" be identified in terms of individual thinkers, or as a history of ideas? Is it an expression of cultural patterns and reflexes? An answer presupposes one's philosophical insight into the particular nature of the individual and into the relationships that distinguish and hold ideas, language, and culture together. The winning of such insight presupposes a certain experience, both in philosophical description and in the analysis of factual occurrences. It is, therefore, a part of the reflective activity of a philosopher as he investigates the historical process in which he and his thoughts participate. Such a theory is necessary in order to write a methodically solid history of philosophy. A certain naiveté is inevitable because the circle we find ourselves in cannot be broken — unless there is an absolute command giving something or someone priority over everything and everyone else. Such a command, in fact, exists: I may not subordinate another individual to anything else. Ideas, language, culture, and all humanity combined do not outweigh one person's worth and dignity. Is there a consequence from this as to who, or what, the true subject of philosophy is? Will a human being no longer deserve respect if his philosophy is not his alone but is rather a product of a particular epoch, society, culture, or language? Can another be taken seriously as a human being if he is not considered an independent, original thinker?

Even without solving the problem just posed, the methodology of the history of philosophy can *begin* by emphasizing the roles that individual philosophers have played in it. This does not make it impossible to qualify their importance as we proceed or to reduce their work to something more fundamental.

Let us begin, then, with reflection on the conditions for a philosophy of history, as constituted by individual thinkers.

The work. A thinker is present for us in the text of his work. As we have seen, this has made itself somehow independent of its author, who has inscribed it into history. As a trace it has its own character and meaning. Does it really *have* a meaning, or does it *receive* one from its readers after the author has let it go? The work is actually to be found between the author and the reader; its meaning is not yet fully determined. But, is it not the reader's task to reconstruct the meaning — the vision and the intentions — expressed in the work? The relation between the reconstruction, or "positivistic" moment, and a creative retaking of the work will be considered later. For the time being we will attend only to the reconstruction of the work's meaning at the time of its writing.

A text. The term *work* is ambiguous. It can include the writer's life work, or *oeuvre*, or it can refer to a single piece of writing. Let us begin with the easiest, which is still difficult: the individual *text* brought forth either orally or in written form. An *orally* presented argument requires time, and it does not necessarily manifest coherence. During its progress the author can question or correct previous assertions, qualify them, and so on. The improvizational character of an oral presentation (not an oral rendition of a preproduced text) has an exciting and unexpected character — at least, if the speaker truly thinks and does not merely repeat old thoughts in a verbal barrage.

A *written* text *can* have a similar temporality — for example, if it is a letter or a journal entry. It differs, however, from an oral presentation in that the writer can review, correct, and change parts of a text before he gives it to his readers. For them, the entire text is present at once. They need time to read it, but this time is ruled by the simultaneity of all phases of the written argument. The art of composition brings temporarily different phases together into one spatial presentation: a book or an article is a compositum pacing and ruling its reader's time. Every reader is, of course, free to break loose from the text's structure, by paging through the book from back to front, for example. But then, he is reading another text. If he wants to know what the author has written, he must follow the author's argument, which leads him by the disposition of signs written in a particular order. Although one can approach it from all sides, a written text has its own disposition, meaning, and order. These must be recognized and formulated clearly by a historian, if he is to say what the text means.

Do the meanings, the structure, and the time-quality of the text correspond to the intentions of its author? One might think that this question is uninteresting — that we have nothing to do with writers but only with what they leave behind. A total distinction between an author and his work, however, makes a meaningful interpretation of his work impossible. As we will see, such a separation destroys our capacity to understand any text. On the other hand, it is not only difficult, or impossible, to discover what thoughts and feelings the author had while writing a text, it is also unnecessary. The text speaks for itself. It is neither a photograph of a human psyche at a given moment nor the expression of a series of internal representations succeeding one another in subjective time. In the text, the author stylizes elements of his and other thinkers' thoughts and experiences, arranging and interpreting them through particular structures. The product is not altogether the author's work. The language and the epic of his time and milieu also speak in it. This does not mean, however, that we can totally ignore the author's life and thought. Through them we arrive at the text's other sources: the author's time, language, and culture. If the author were a mere exponent or symptom, he would be only a medium. But a complete reduction of a thinker to anonymous patterns of language and culture contradicts the essence of language, which imposes at least some responsibility on its "user."

The rendition of what a text "wants to say" takes place on at least two levels. Historians who see philosophy as a stream of views note agreements and differences among thinkers' opinions during the same or different periods. The pensive responding to posed and to-be-posed questions, through the analyses and argumentation characteristic of philosophy, is not what is dealt with in such a catalogue of opinions and conceptions. A history sensitive to the genuine activity of philosophy concentrates on its characteristic ways of questioning and responding. It tries to reveal the inner consistency, or inconsistency, of various positions, the explicit arguments and the harmonies and discords hidden in their presuppositions, and the inspiration giving birth to the work.

The coherence of a text can be characterized in several ways. The coherence of a poem is different from that of a scientific treatise. The most fundamental structure of a philosophical text can be called the "logic" of the text (we use the term *logic* in a very broad sense). Now it is utter naivete to think we can, or should, possess the only true logic, which will enable us to ascertain and judge the (in)coherence of texts. Every text has its own logic, and the question of correct coherence can be inappropriate if more than one "true" logic is possible. It is naive to believe that all possible logics have been formulated, or can be formulated, within the framework of "modern logic." The various versions of "modern logic" are founded on numerous logical and ontological presuppositions, which need justification in a discussion of philosophy's fundamental questions. These fundamental questions are not purely formal because they already imply a certain notion of truth — and thus a certain theory on the nature of knowledge and reality, and their relation.

The peculiar logic of a philosophical text is twofold. Each text upholds a certain logical ideal. The writer is led by an idea of argumentation, a legitimate way of proceeding, and so on. The resulting "objective" structures represent a second, actual logic; they do not necessarily correspond to the ideal for which the writer is striving. The logic actually practiced can fall short of the ideal. But it can also be better: for example, through a breakthrough that is more intuitive than reflective, which leads to new possibilities for language and thought that can later become normative in the formulation of new logical ideas and ideals.

A good rendition of a philosophical text requires a precise analysis of the logical ideal and the logic attained in it. All structural elements must be discovered and illuminated as they are. Every text has a structure of its own: the most original texts are characterized by a fundamental and thorough restructuring of the usual automatisms of definition, divisions, and composition. This is why the logics of Spinoza's *Ethics*, Kant's *Critique of Pure Reason*, Hegel's *Encyclopedia*, and Nietzsche's *On the Genealogy of Morals* are so different and are irreducible to one another. No logician can subjugate them with a supreme judgment, although the great and small Russells try to do so, time and time again.

As pointed out, the peculiar logic of a text does not constitute the most fundamental level of discourse it sets forth, even if it paves the way to that level. Aside from the structure, the text's particular *style* points to the primary source of its life — its specific relation to truth and reality, its peculiar "ontology."

An oeuvre. The fundamental ontology, whether professed or realized, may be approached from the perspective of anthropological and existential analysis, relating the studied *work* to the living thought and *life* of its author. Before we turn to this approach, a few words may be said about the plurality of writings making up an *oeuvre.*

The analysis and interpretation of a single work is insufficient to characterize its writer. A production of successive texts results in a simultaneity of books, which can be read in any order and with different purposes. From the "positivistic" perspective, two lines of interpretation are possible and recommended. If one lays out all the works of an author side by side, they constitute a whole whose meaning and interconnection must be discovered. If they form one self-consistent system, this *oeuvre* can be explained in a way similar to the explanation of a single work. Often, however, the various parts of an *oeuvre* cannot be thought into a harmony because each asks radically different questions, or even contradicting ones. The differences in singular works must be described and understood, without neglecting the genuine or apparent contradictions they introduce into the whole. The differences sometimes reveal a fundamental lack of clarity. A lack of awareness of underlying questions and prejudices, for example, can lead to contradictions. The explanation often also lies in the author's correction, explicit or not, of thoughts expressed in earlier works. A genetic interpretation deals with the genesis of an *oeuvre* and attempts to reconstruct the development, of which the successive texts are junction points. Such a reconstruction is not a psychologically accurate description of what an author thinks and feels throughout his philosophical activity but is rather a schematic rendering of the main arguments from one work to another. Of course, it is not sufficient for one to construct a plausible argument whereby the ideas of one work can be transformed into those of another, because the truthful description of a historical genesis is based and depends on objective indications in the text itself, from manuscripts, remarks, and other data gathered from the thought and life of the author. If these are not given, the reconstruction can resort to hypothetical explanations to bridge gaps. But a thinker's development does not always proceed in a logical and obvious way. It can also obey less rational, emotional, and violent motives.

Work and life. Now we come to an approach that does not limit itself to individual texts and their interrelations but explicitly takes the author's *life* into account to give a genetic and systematic interpretation of his philosophy.

A philosopher's life includes nonphilosophical and nonrational factors, that, together with the philosophical elements, constitute and define his individual history. To what extent can a philosophy be understood through the philosopher's life history? What is the value of biographies in the rendition of philosophy?

The distinction between the experiential and conceptual totality of a philosophy and its logical structure may help in finding the extent to which a body of thought is the sediment of a life. Obviously, the *opinions* of philosophers are effects of their lives, upbringing, environment, and experience. The originality of a unique life forms the all-inclusive viewpoint from which the individual sees reality. Although I can respect other perspectives and improve my own by relating to them, as an individual I do not have another point of view. Because I am this particular individual with this particular life history, the objects I think about and my methods of investigation are partially set. Must we go further and say that even the logical elements on which my argumentations rely are subject to the contingencies marking me as this person, of this milieu and this time? Does *haecceitas* govern the deepest foundations of thinking? But how can we maintain the universality of thinking? Do we not lose the idea of justification if every system stands or falls on the individual peculiarities from which it derives its inner logic? Can and must a philosopher only speak to those who are closely related to him? Properly speaking, such would not be possible if one seriously considered individuality as the inevitable starting point. Philosophy would disintegrate into an unlimited number of monads, all thinking for themselves. They would not be able to justify their thoughts to themselves, for what kind of justification can lack a superindividual standard of truth? The very idea of coherence and the demand for noncontradiction cannot be salvaged after such an abolition of universality, not even through arbitrary definitions. These, too, become impossible if one does not presuppose any logical universality.

Can thinking outwit the influences determining an individual's outlook by submitting it to analysis and critique? Philosophizing would have no significance if it were totally impossible to get a critical grasp of the social, cultural, and psychic factors framing an individual life. It would be suicidal for a philosophy to maintain that it was a mere effect of purely extraphilosophical elements. Its claim would be destroyed in the discovery of its impossibility. A history of philosophy would subsequently only be possible as a series of reports on philosophical wholes as products of *non*philosophical factors. Thinking would then have no history of its own.

A philosopher's experience is otherwise. He does not necessarily see himself as a king of thought — the thought of lordship may even be repulsive to him — but he cannot be a mere pawn of irrational factors either. His awareness of himself as a relatively autonomous producer of thoughts is not a sufficient argument against the conception that he is such a pawn or effect. For how can he refute the idea that his evidence is the effect of a deepseated illusion? How can he prove that his is not a false consciousness? The Marxist, psychoanalytic, and structuralist distrust of the essence of philosophy cannot be refuted by simply referring to self-evident experiences. The difference between true and untrue experiences is at home in philosophy, just as is the truth that great efforts and various conversions are necessary to correct the evidence of initial experiences. On the other hand, the specialists of suspicion tread on thin ice when they ground their unmasking in a conviction that is peculiar to them. According to their own theories, all such principles as "the unconscious," "language," "culture," "education," and economic or other infrastractures are at least as dubious as is thinking when it claims to lay down basic rules and to discover fundamental truths. All sciences, undermining the basic intention of philosophy by seeing it as a derivative function, share this same basic intention. They do this more dogmatically because philosophy is more circumspect. By declaring the truth of philosophy to be illusory, psychoanalysis, linguistics, ethnology, sociology, and history all proclaim themselves to be metaphilosophical, or supraphilosophical. But metaphilosophy and supra- or transphilosophy are parts of philosophy! If a science presumes to give metaphilosophical judgments, it makes itself ridiculous, unless it recognizes philosophy. For philosophers are specialists at laying foundations, truth, reality, appearance, and unmasking. If antiphilosophers believe they have discovered a more radical way of asking the old questions of truth and appearance, they must prove this before the forum of philosophy. If they are successful, the history of philosophy will have reached a new milestone. A science cannot fight against philosophy unless it develops philosophical procedures strong enough to compete with the best procedures of existing philosophies.

The presentation of a philosophical *oeuvre* demands not only a faithful reconstruction of its empirical and logical peculiarities but also a clarification of the ties binding it to the life of the author. Not everything in a philosopher's life is important for the form and content of his thought, but if his philosophizing has the seriousness and depth of a wager with life itself, a historian cannot disregard the way in which his texts match his particular life, how they come forth from it, and what repercussions they have on it. A general theory of the relation between life and thought is perhaps not possible, considering that this relation *in concreto* involves the unique way in which an individual philosopher lives and thinks. If it becomes thorough and serious, thinking is not separable from fear and hope, willing and desiring.

The discussion of all scientific ways of reducing a philosophy to something else can be done in a positive manner by considering the life of an individual thinker as a way of discovering more truth. Such a way is not necessarily rectilinear; it may lead to insoluble problems, and even to defeat. However, it is still philosophical so long as it is governed by a passion for the truth. Whatever is unmasked as a lie or an illusion may perhaps also be understood as an unsuccessful attempt to see more genuinely how things really are. A philosopher is aided by his most suspicious enemies, because they force him to become more genuine. True experience is not a common fact, but rather an ideal. Every demystification bears fruit if it leads to the conversion of the unmasked. By leaps and turns, a philosopher becomes more true. The way of enlightenment is a way of purification. Philosophizing is *a way of becoming true*. But it does not stand on its own, independent of how the philosopher exists and relates to other persons and things. Truth does not deliver itself to an abstract, uprooted thought; it rather makes way for itself at the most genuine and truest "level," where the meaning of life is realized.

A good rendition of a philosophy includes a biography of the thinker clearly delineating how his philosophy is interwoven with his existential search for truth. This level lies much deeper than what is empirically-logically reconstructable. The existential perspective from which a philosophical *oeuvre* is considered does not treat it as a piece of literature or as pure expression; the lived discovery of truths neither abolishes nor replaces their argumentative justification. The difference between a history of philosophy trying to understand the relation between life and philosophical thought and one ignoring the existential context is the more concrete notion of truth in the former. The human significance of a particular philosophy disappears when the ideas of which it is composed are isolated from the life experiment upon which its author has ventured, not only — and not primarily — by his philosophizing but also by his living a thoughtful life. This experiment is the true *experience* that ought to be revealed if we want to know the true meaning of a philosophical *oeuvre*.

To explain a philosophy, then, means not only unfolding it at the level of interconnected concepts but also showing how it emerges as one element from an individual history. A great difficulty with such an explanation is that one must reveal it from the perspective of the author's own claims and motivations, without subjecting it to foreign (e.g., to my) schemas. By subordinating the works of other thinkers to a superconnection coming from me, I distort their meaning. As dictator, I manipulate them as parts of my conceptual realm. What Plato says about a tyrant may be applied here: if my dealings

with texts become violent, I will become extremely poor because
they will only teach me what fits into the framework to which I am
accustomed. They will either agree with my opinions or they will
contradict them, but my reading is useless with regard to the task of
the search for truth. Explaining a philosophy means reviving
another's thoughts, motivations, and experiences. I must work my
way into his text and be its soul and apologist. Its logical coherence
is easily rendered, even though we have seen that singularity already
plays a role at the level of logic. The reconstruction of fundamental
experiences and perspectives, basic intuitions, presuppositions, and
motives makes the greatest demands on the historian, because it
requires the combination of two attitudes difficult to bring together:
on the one hand the historian's interest must be captivated by the
works under consideration and on the other, a certain distance from
his preferences is necessary in order to become receptive to their
originality. A historian's quality is determined by the unity of openness and philosophical engagement he achieves. Here, too, greatness
is equal to space times depth.

6.4.2. Milieu and Time

Our initial objective stance towards a philosophical text,
without considering the philosopher's life history, is made more concrete by reflecting on the relation between life and textual production. The concentration on a philosopher and his *oeuvre* is, however,
still an abstraction. A more concrete consideration asks how the
philosopher is related to his milieu and time. Is it possible to be
"ahead of one's time"? Are there philosophers who are above the
culture wherein they are raised? Or, is every philosopher an exponent of a given situation and epoch?

Just as the relation of life to work provokes a philosophical
theory interweaving thinking and existence, so must a philosophy of
history, sensitive to the nonindividual aspects of philosophizing,
thematize the relation of a philosopher's life and work on the one
hand and the historical *context* encompassing them on the other. An
integral history of philosophy includes substantial contributions
from social, political, economic, and cultural history, natural and
social geography, sociology, cultural anthropology, and so forth.
Even a systematic philosophy cannot ignore the nonphilosophical

study of philosophy presented by the various positive sciences. While their lessons can never replace philosophy's self-understanding, they provide us with considerations necessary for an insight into the roots of our own thought. A philosophical history of philosophy, however, is very different from an economic, psychoanalytic, or political interpretation of the philsophical works and traditions confronting us. The history of contemporary, and earlier, philosophizing can be presented as a series of adventures in the history of power, or as effects of socioeconomic processes. Such presentations probably have their own scientific truth, but as soon as they claim to give fundamental explanations (i.e., as soon as they presume to make philosophical claims), they degenerate into a form of positivism by absolutizing their relative viewpoints. A philosophically oriented history of philosophy (and *a fortiori* a thematic philosophy accounting for its own past) does not allow its domination by psychoanalytic, sociological, or other scientific reductions, although it seriously considers them in assessing their impact on original experience and thought processes resulting in a thematic philosophy. The various ways that social scientists use to show that a philosophy is a conscious or unconscious expression of something other than the experience and thinking of its author, along with the demystifications reducing many thoughts to illusions and lies, provide a lover of truth with food for thought. The task of unmasking has been known in philosophy since the beginning of its history. From the time of Heraclitus and Parmenides, all great philosophers have understood every thought process as a navigation between appearance and reality. The (relative) truth and value of reductions to nonphilosophical elements have also been known. The problem they posed coincides with the (old) philosophical question of the difference between the basic and other levels of being human, or with the question of the essence of humanness and culture. We do not have a ready-made scheme for integrating scientific unmaskings or reductions — the tempting scheme of freedom's mastering the factors that simultaneously limit and make it possible is itself under discussion — but, a naive absolutizing of the viewpoints mentioned is just as shortsighted as a quick recuperation. A sign of this naiveté is the scepticism that necessarily results from such an absolutization: if everything is will to power, repression, class consciousness, or the like, the idea of science and *a fortiori* philosophy no longer has any meaning, except of some kind of irrationality. Consequently, it makes no sense to argue, unless one is bold enough to forge weapons out of false and unprovable thoughts.

Time is the universal horizon spanning the geographical and social milieu, technological and economic structures and processes, cultural levels, trends and events, idioms of language, commonplaces, popular opinions, traditions, and expectations. How is a philosophical work related to its time and milieu? To what extent is it an exponent of the material, social, artistic, and ideological processes in that atmosphere? How is it related to the "consciousness" of its time?

An analysis of such a time consciousness should involve distinctions revealing the plurality within this consciousness. "The people," the various social classes, intellectuals, semi-intellectuals, journalists, "the elite," scientists, politicians, governments, and philosophers vary in what they consider obvious, ordinary, proper, worthwhile, and characteristic for "our time." Can the differences in their consciousness be understood as modifications of one overall "collective consciousness"? Or, does this term merely refer to similar aspects of a large number of group and individual forms of consciousness? Without doubt, all or most works written in the same period have a certain affinity with one another. In certain respects, even the exceptions (e.g. those "ahead of their time") can be understood as exponents of their time. The "spirit" that inspires these works can be recognized, allowing historians to group them within a specific period. Although there are many affinities overlapping certain periods — for example, many Catholics in the 1930s felt closer to the medieval Church than to modern democracy, and many contemporary philosophers are more Platonist than structuralist — avant-gardists, as well as archconservatives, are "children of their time." Epigones and traditionalists glance back at the former times; their styles are mixtures of the past and the present. Nor do revolutionaries or prophets escape the power and spirit of the times against which they revolt. They struggle, here and now, against other elements of the "here and now." Their time is a battlefield of tensions and contradictions. The "spirit of their time" expresses itself in a multiplicity of divergent movements. Instead of a static present, it is a history.

To establish a satisfactory method for the history of philosophy, we need to solve the following problems: (1) To what extent can we understand the works of a philosopher as expressions of the life and thought of his time? (2) What does "life and thought of his time" mean? Which levels of life (economic, social, cultural, etc.) and which levels of thought (everyday, scientific, philosophical, religious) must be differentiated here, and how do they relate to one another? (3) What is the place and function of this philosophical *oeuvre* with regard to the other elements and the spirit of its time?

The third question coincides with the first one but is formulated in a different manner, by integrating it with the second question. These problems can only be answered through an integral analysis of particular time periods, including a philosophical consideration of philosophical history as well as a general social and historical theory. It is impossible for one person to perform this task; interdisciplinary research is necessary. Usually a historian of philosophy repeats customary schemes without much ado.

Certain elements in the context of a philosophical *oeuvre* are more or less philosophical in nature: genuine or supposed self-evident truths, conceptual presuppositions, current language games, and standard questions provide an unavoidable grounding for thought, even when it turns against them. A philosopher is someone who draws upon the tendencies and trends of his time to form questions and ideas in his own characteristic, and often "untimely," way. If he succeeds, he transforms the customs of thought into a new whole, whose meaning can be defended in its own right.

6.4.3. PHILOSOPHICAL CONSTELLATIONS

Although great philosophers are not many, every period in history has a few. Even though they match one another in quality, however, their conceptions and logic can be radically different. Even if all philosophies emerge from different sources, do they not have a certain affinity? The constellations formed by philosophers of a certain period suggest at least the following questions: (1) How are the individual philosophers related to one another? (2) How are they related to the philosophical, the semiphilosophical and the prephilosophical traditions of their time? and (3) Can the individual philosophies and philosophical trends of one historical period be brought together in one all-encompassing characteristic of "the philosophy" or the philosophical "spirit" of this period?

These questions can be formulated differently and further analyzed. One can, for example, more sharply distinguish between individual philosophies, schools of thought, and philosophically relevant undercurrents to determine the prevailing experiences, language patterns, argumentative structures, and so forth for each of these. A complete theory of the history of philosophy is impossible without a systematic analysis of all the elements involved in these questions. The main question at this stage of our reflection, however, is: Is it possible to take all the philosophical trends and tendencies of a certain period into the concept of "the philosophy of a period" (e.g., of the Renaissance or of 1780–1830)? Is a superindividual totality of a temporal nature possible, or is an individual work, wherein a thinker collects manifold material and influences by transforming them into one unique textual whole, the highest unity? Or, does the highest philosophical synthesis exist in the philosopher himself, when seen as one life of thought in which the works are merely marking stones left behind along a journey?

Which schema is appropriate in understanding the interrelation of philosophies in one period of history? Must one not possess a superphilosophy to bring those philosophies together into one constellation? If their authors are truly fundamental thinkers, their philosophies are themselves such a first (and last) or superphilosophy, which cannot bear rivals. The concepts *affinity* and *enmity* might allow more freedom than *synthesis* or *refutation*. What is the difference between a 'constellation' and a 'synthesis'? How does a historian escape the temptation of making himself the only metaphilosopher, leaving all other philosophers behind and beneath him? Does the only solution lie in his abandonment of historical "objectivity"? Must he boldly state that he is not interested in a rendition of earlier philosophies but merely concerned with what he, as a thinker, can do with them? In this case, the history of philosophy is only a preparation for a well-informed thematic philosophy in which others offer the material and, perhaps, the inspiration.

a. The unity of an *oeuvre*. The question of how contemporary thinkers can be grouped together is part of the question of whether superindividual wholes can be differentiated in the history of philosophy. In a single work, we seek the inner unity and connection of a text unfolding in time; to discover its structure, we have to go back and forth from a to z. Taken together, several works of an author form a philosophical *oeuvre*. In some cases, an *oeuvre* can be understood as one ongoing text. A succession of works, however, usually attests to changes a philosopher goes through in the course of time. Temporality and a special way of coming to be are part of the totality of an *oeuvre*. No ready-made schema can characterize the development of this totality, because each has its own genesis and temporal coherence. If one still wishes to speak of an all-encompassing text, present here and now as a range of books, one must not forget the particular time structure differentiating these texts into phases. The commentary must not only display its thematic consistency but also tell a story.

The rendition of an *oeuvre* is not a simplified copy of a writer's mental life. The development of his thought — the same may be said *a fortiori* for his life — is more complicated than we can know from published texts. An author relates only a few of the stages of his life and thought in his works, only a few of his achievements. Unspoken and unconscious thoughts and motives can be revealed by the detective skills of exegetes, psychoanalysts, literary critics, and other analytic specialists. However, the philosophical meaning of an *oeuvre* is in the specific way it has transformed all the vital factors into an explicit body of thought.

The life of a philosopher presents itself as an inclusive totality within which philosophizing can be defined. However, objections can be raised against summarizing a philosophy by encircling its author's life. *First* of all, we are not concerned with his life, but rather with the philosophy that comes out of it. The moment his works are produced, when living thoughts are transformed into objective elements belonging to our cultural "apparatus," they attain independence from their writer. *Second*, a philosopher's birth and death do not coincide with the beginning and end of his philosophical, or philosophically relevant, developments. Thus, *third* (and this is closely related to the previous point), the path of thinking is not a copy of the life in which it takes place. Extensive psychological and philosophical analyses are necessary to elucidate the complicated network connecting the nontheoretical motives of a life and the philosophical production it leaves behind. But even before such analyses, it seems plausible that the totality, the structure, and the genesis of the *theoretical* do not completely coincide with the totality, the structure, and the genesis of the *lived* life. A historian of philosophy is therefore more cautious if he starts with the study of the *oeuvre* as a closed theoretical totality, without immediately questioning the relation of this *oeuvre* to the life from which it springs. While at least some acquaintance with its existential sources is demanded for the concrete understanding of a philosophy, at the beginning this can be intuitive and unscientific.

A *fourth* reason why the works and the life of a great philosopher are not coextensive is that most of the teaching contained in the work is posthumous: it has another time and future, distinct from the life of the thinker. The works become a property of other times. The meaning that a good interpretation can acquire from them inevitably changes.

We must not be deluded by the apparent unity of a philosophical *oeuvre*. For some authors, even works intended for publication are missing; for others, we have all the experiments and finger exercises they themselves had discarded. Must we count the posthumous papers as part of an author's *oeuvre*, or should we be merciful enough not to identify a philosopher such as Kant with the literary stammerings that he left behind? The works written are, to a great extent, a matter of chance: the demands of teaching, questions from students, invitations and calls for papers, the successes of rivals, imposters, sophists, and trends all play a role in the production of texts. The idea that the work of a great thinker can be read as one interconnected whole is thus too perfect (i.e., too abstractly philosophical) to be true. But it is useful, and inevitable, in a philosophical rendition of the history of philosophy.

b. The unity of a period.   The difficulties of totalizing become greater when a historian tries to create connections among the various philosophies of a certain period. What unity can bring the various philosophers and their works together in one philosophical whole? Or, is this a wrong question? Must we seek the unity of a philosophical period at the level of philosophically relevant currents and undercurrents? Do such things as *periods* in "the life of philosophy" actually exist?

Taking available texts as our starting points, we might consider whether a philosophical period can be described and understood as a Con-text, of which all surviving texts are fragments. In spite *and* because of their differences (which may contain contradictions), these fragments belong together in a manner open to further analysis. It seems possible to circumscribe a philosophy by characterizing its texts and their textual connections (without trying to hide, polish, or remove their contradictions by one's own synthesis).

An objection to reducing all past philosophies into one text of texts, or supertext, is that it treats these as a series of corpses. As soon as a text ceases to be thought, it is dead. The thought possibilities it harbors do not come to life unless someone (re)thinks them. A philosophy of the past exists just like today's philosophy, here and now, when it is thought by one or more thinkers. A philosophy "of the past" differs from one "of our time," however, because it is *rethought* via interpretation. It needs at least two human beings in order to exist: the writer, whose life no longer participates in history, and the reader, who did not live in the writer's time. Readers are presupposed when texts are written. The chronological difference between a dead writer and a living reader means that the former can no longer defend his text; he needs others to plead his case. As opposed to a text, a Context is not produced by a philosopher as his own thought: it comes to be when someone else takes the texts of several philosophers together, in a diagnostic synthesis. Such a synthesis forms a metatext, displaying the connections of a textual constellation. An insight into such connections is hardly possible for one of the thinkers functioning *within* this constellation. He gives an interpretation of other texts and productions of his period from his particular perspective. A later reader has more distance; his description of the earlier context is marked by a new perspective, which is determined by his place within a later constellation. Rethinking gives old texts a new place and meaning within a new context: the written and spoken thinking of another time. Like the old text, its retaking has its own history, too. It can be forgotten, scorned, refuted, refined, or amended. The history of texts is a history of libraries and archives, revived only when thinking takes a new turn. An earlier philosophy remains a fossil, until someone is able to read and understand it well.

The question of characterizing an earlier Context (i.e., the designation of periods in the history of philosophy) may perhaps be formulated as follows:

It seems possible to read the most important texts of a certain period and to distinguish them according to content, form, and style. (The definition and selection of the "important" ones, of course, pose enormous problems, but we will leave this problem for the moment.) The constellation of the (questionable) selection of texts presents us with the task of describing and interpreting its nature, structure, and style. Such characterization is even more questionable than the interpretation of a single work. From the corner of the present (where I do not even have an "objective" view of my own relation to other contemporary people) and within the web of a specific context spun around me, I give my limited vision of thoughts inscribed into the documents of an earlier present. A "period of philosophy" is an interpretation only existing as part of a later context, from which an earlier one acquires one of its meanings. An insight into the constellation within which a thinker develops his thoughts cannot be adequately attained by someone within the same constellation. The question of characterizing the pattern of a particular period can only be answered in that period through risky suppositions. Good overviews come later, which are to a large extent determined by later patterns' interpreting the earlier one. The characteristics of a period also have a history: the meaning of an earlier Context depends on a historical interpretation functioning within a later Context, which in turn points beyond itself for a better diagnosis of the past.

c. The unity of a history. The problem of a superindividual historical totality becomes yet more difficult when we reflect on history as a continuous shifting of transitory constellations. Some levels of history change very slowly, but in the history of philosophy, most changes occur very rapidly. Closer consideration may reveal a slower movement underneath those changes, or even a total standstill for several centuries — for example, when certain assumptions are accepted and unquestioned for a very long time. However, there are always important differences at less fundamental levels.

A total history of philosophical thought is not possible. One can surmise that the differences between traditions will diminish in the further unification of our world and that it will be possible someday, owing to enormous simplifications and distortions, to give the same overgeneralizing synthesis of philosophical world history as is given in our time of "Western" philosophy. A *world history of philosophy*, as opposed to a socioeconomic world history, is impossible. While the concept and theory of non-Western economics are also Western products, a history submitting Oriental and other philosophies to the fundamental problems, schemas, and concepts of Western philosophy will miss its target before it even begins. The non-Western philosophies it will treat can provide nothing but confirmations, variations, or denials of typical elements in the Western tradition. They will not be allowed to show their own character. A genuine world history of philosophy has to portray the constellations and movements of radically different traditions by simultaneously revealing their profound strangeness to one another as well as certain affinities justifying their joining under the title of "philosophy."

A *history of Western philosophy* is difficult enough. It is also not possible without enormous simplification and scarely justifiable universalizations. Philosophers, works, currents, and undercurrents do not reveal their secrets in labels and hasty characterizations. The precise rendition of a philosophy presupposes that one has spent a long time studying it. But how can one individual work through the whole of Western philosophy with its multiformity and constant mobility? The historian's remembering, which gathers the many expressions together, changes the past into elements of his own thought. Selectivity, the neglect of important authors, and the misrepresentation of earlier thoughts are lesser dangers to one who wants to profit from our heritage for his creative thought alone than they are to a true historian. However, a history of philosophy is not the same as a propaedeutic phenomenology of the visions whose spirit can make us wiser. As we have seen, self-education based on history is not only an *anamnesis*, but an exodus and alienation as well. An emphasis on this last aspect does not abolish the difference between philosophical formation and the history of philosophy.

Without a standpoint transcending all philosophies and their histories, and without identifying himself with a particular position within the different constellations, a historian must describe their simultaneity and continuous transformations. At the same time he must integrate the interwovenness of every philosophy with its author's prephilosophical experiences and with the philosophical, psychical, social, economic, technical, and cultural histories in which it is rooted.

Such a history is very different from a history of ideas maintaining that ideas lead an independent life apart from other histories. Ideas neither exist nor function except as elements within thinking individuals' materially and socially rooted lives. Ideas and ideologies certainly have power, but they are not independent substances isolated in their ideality. They cannot be understood in isolation from their thinkers.

The history of philosophy also differs from a history of ideology that reduces all ideas and philosophies to struggles for property and power or for love. Although certain philosophical criticisms of ideologies may be true, they overextend themselves when they claim to be more than just one (interesting, but partial) contribution to the problematic of truth and appearance. By ascertaining the truth, they refute their own claim. Absolutizing their viewpoint condemns such criticisms to a greater naiveté than that of the criticized philosophies. The latter at least know that scientific analyses cannot answer philosophical questions.

A complete history of philosophy must not only be concerned with reconstructing the different philosophers' key positions, shifts, and developments but must also be aware of their influences upon their own and other times, of their literary traces, the use and abuse of their thoughts, of legal and economic institutions stimulated by their theories, and so on. For a philosopher writing philosophy's history, this presupposes a thematic philosophy of the total culture as well as its material and social foundations.

6.5 Dogmatism and hermeneutics

From the foregoing, a number of critical remarks regarding the traditional rendition of philosophy follows.

The "positivism" defended here condemns every history of philosophy with pretensions to "objectivity," yet with an explicit or implicit apology for a particular philosophy. Thomistic histories that view all philosophy before Aquinas as preparation and all philosophy after him as elaborations of his doctrine or as decline are as bad as Marxist, Hegelian, or empiricist histories. The writer proclaims one star as the all-encompassing synthesis of all the constellations and movements of history.

Do I not contradict here the demand for a historian of philosophy to be a philosopher himself and for writing philosophy in the light of actual thematic problems? How else can distance and engagement be unified, without choosing a position and paying the price of one-sidedness so as to avoid an illusory objectivism so neutral that it cannot say anything interesting about the history of thought?

A one-sided and apologetic account of my personal past has every right to be. It is a genealogy of my family and my friends, acquaintances, and enemies. However, it is not a history of philosophy.

We can extend the perspective of an "I" to the perspective of a group — a "we." But even then "our" history of philosophy will be no more than a partial plea. If such apologies make universal claims, they degenerate into imperialism and colonialism.

Is a nonimperialistic, nondogmatic, and nontriumphant attitude possible with respect to human history? The metalevel forced on the historian by his design demands its own legitimation. This produces a peculiar (meta)philosophy. As historian I have my own metaphilosophy, whether disguised within a history of philosophy or not. Does my explicit or implicit metaphilosophy provide enough room for the understanding of all the philosophies presented in my history in their proper light? Among them are other explicit and implicit metaphilosophies. Does the metaphilosophy of a historian leave the other philosophies and metaphilosophies free? Can I be so "democratic" as to recognize their equal status, worth, or even truth? Based on what has been said so far, a complete answer cannot be given. The following discussion will return to this question. However, it is clear at this point that the idea of an "impartial" history demands as many parties as there are actual philosophies and possible metaphilosophies.

Subtler ways of making an apology can be found in accounts composed according to schemas of rise and fall or of unending progress. They assume that ideas can be attained once and for all; their authors are convinced that they possess the criteria that can distinguish true from false philosophies. Just as hopeless are those histories that regard no one position as more important than another. The thematic *defeatism* evident in such indifference is the opposite of an equally bad apologetic *dogmatism*.

The inquiry into historical wholes in the life of philosophy necessarily presents us with the thematic problems of *absolutism* and *relativism*, and with the basic questions concerning *truth* and *time*. On our present level, where the monologic model still prevails, overcoming partiality seems impossible. Many argue that since we cannot reach "*objectivity*," a *subjective* viewpoint is the beginning and end of all truth and method. In view of justice, however, the choice for a subjective perspective is unfair and weak. Even from a monological viewpoint, I am defeated if I cannot say how the history of philosophical multiplicity *really* fits together as a whole. As long as my ideal is the true rendition of actual history, in which my viewpoint is only one possibility, the partiality of my vision is a makeshift measure, perhaps a necessary step, that must be overcome later. The idea of a neutral rendition is an illusion, but the "positivism" shown here as a necessity remains a criterion. As a regulatory idea, it must be combined with the necessity of developing my version of philosophical history as an exciting movement of constellations sweeping me along with it. Both the personal retrieval of past and present philosophies and a certain positivism are necessary for the sake of truth and justice. The retrieval can be narrow or open. But it will always be characterized by a particular vision and style. The limitation of its thematic perspective does not guarantee a fruitful way of bringing dead texts to life, but it is a necessary condition if those texts are to say anything at all. The strength of a hermeneutical relationship with the past rests not only on its exciting or dazzling results but also on the impossibility of another method. All "objective," positivistic, and ideological accounts are disguised forms of hermeneutics. Their weakness is in the naiveté of their claim to the contrary (and thus they dispute, ignore, or despise the hermeneutical method).

At this point, the meaning of a hermeneutical approach is still an egological one. Other philosophers exist for me. They are master, friend, challenge, source of contention or inspiration. Of course I do not want to be unjust to them, but I am not their apologist. My defense of their thoughts is strategic in the expansion of my own consciousness: I become wiser through different and dangerous discussions. By struggling with others, I discover and (re)form the tradition(s) to which I belong. Thus, history changes, confirms, and illustrates my own philosophy. Others can read "the" (their) history differently: they have every right to do so. The history of philosophy exists as a diversity of stories. The totality of all stories replaces the historical overviews for which only one author is responsible.

How can the unity-in-diversity of such a totality be understood? Is the history of philosophy divided into a Babel of subjective genealogies containing as many disparate viewpoints as there are *now* philosophical positions?

A *hermeneutic* history of philosophy is a genealogical tree set up by an interpreter honoring his family. It is not necessary for him to be a follower of that direction, because one can also write a family history out of affection and interest. Hermeneutics does not exclude distance and reserve. It gives up the vain notion of the Great Synthesis and travels a more fruitful path: the explanation of our past does not begin at the end of or above history; it continues one or more traditions and is part of them. A hermeneutical reading knows that it itself is a new, yet not completely new, part of history. Such a history of philosophy is a fragment of a systematic philosophy, which in this case is not directly expressed in a thematic way, but via resurrections of related thinkers and enemies.

Bad hermeneutics coincides with a dogmatic form of positivism. Epigones who interpret the entire history of philosophy as a collection of preparations, mistakes, variations, shadows, and consequences of one truth are often quite successful. Their readers understand what is set before them. The doctrine is clear. The confidence of propagandists can make a great impression. Although their efforts allow the dissemination of great thoughts, their influence is harmful because they hinder the unfolding of genuine thought and so destroy the heart of the admirable systems advertised by them.

The question may arise: Why is the idea that the true way of thinking has been found and only needs repetition, elaboration, and appropriation so unacceptable? It would be acceptable if our thinking could go beyond time and look down on history from an unlimited vantage point. A "history of thought" would then mean that an adulthood had been attained, making all preliminary and subsequent stages superfluous. There would be room only for application and translation. However, although perfection as an ideal beckons from the horizon, the history of philosophy is a history of searching and approaching. But in that case, no one can use the "only true philosophy" as a standard for deciding the meaning of the various existing philosophies.

If every interpretation of the "history of philosophy" is only fragmentary and "subjective," every version of it is only one among many partly complementary, partly opposed versions legitimizing themselves from other viewpoints and traditions. Aware of this fact, I go in a formal way beyond my own perspective. A question inevitably arises: are *all* interpretations equally legitimate? What truth or untruth comes forth in the totality of all possible versions of the history of philosophy, in its parts and as a whole? The demand for an all-inclusive viewpoint, the positing and the formal, empty thinking of the total truth, is unavoidable. But perhaps we are mistaken in trying to solve this problem by the grace of a superinterpretation including and overpowering all possible interpretations. The desire for a monologue in which all apologies receive their ultimate coherence ignores the temporal and cultural limits of our insight. Is such a breakthrough possible? Does it make sense to speak of a *species aeternitatis*, of a timeless or "eternal" truth? It is not difficult to admit that we cannot unfold such a truth to its full extent. (It is uncertain whether or not this lack of pretension is a sign of modesty.) But, can we forget the idea of an ultimate and absolute truth? Can we stop desiring it? Or, more importantly, can we continue to philosophize if we altogether eliminate this idea?

Another perspective impresses itself on us: how far can we extend the temporal and topical limitation of our thinking, perhaps even overcome it, by thematizing the intersubjective and social conditions that determine truth-seeking speech? Does a good history of philosophy, like a thematic philosophy, require us to turn from monologue to dialogue?

Chapter III

Philosophy as Discussion

What is the relation between philosophy and its history? What consequences does the answer have for both? Chapter 2 developed this question from the fact (which was also a demand) that thematic philosophizing always begins with, and remains, learning. Complete knowledge is not possible in philosophy: this is an unattainable ideal. The questions philosophy asks are too difficult. They go beyond the boundaries of our capacity for insight. But for this same reason they always lead us back to the company of thinkers who have labored at these boundaries.

In the preceding chapter, *others* were discussed as predecessors, examples, and writers of texts, that "I," the eternal beginner, receive, read, digest, appropriate, retake, and prolong. Other philosophers were there *for me*. The perspective was hermeneutic and egological. Spoken and written words were important for my development as a philosopher. They were signposts and guidelines; they made me aware of an inheritance that could enrich me if I fulfilled certain conditions.

The study of philosophy is, however, not only listening and learning, repeating, and reflecting, it is also thinking and speaking ahead, for the sake of others who want to think. Every speech aiming at truth is an attempt to bring others something worthwhile to think about. Even the clumsiest utterance makes such claims. Learning to speak is learning to teach. A training in philosophy is unsuccessful if the pupil becomes an epigone. Philosophical parrots miss the quintessence of thought; only dictators can find satisfaction in them. The professor who bears no opposition, the Party or Church that knows everything, the Movement that forces solidarity through slogans: all these are caricatures and enemies of true philosophy. A true philosopher eventually provokes others to criticism and opposition. If they do not emancipate themselves from their teacher's authority, there is no hope for any communication in which both will be the other's pupil and master. The Socrates of Plato's dialogues is not a good example. There is not much left for his interlocutors to say except "Yes, of course" (or "No, of course not"). The real Socrates was better, for he brought forth Plato, and Plato brought forth Aristotle. Finding one's own path of thought comes not only from having good teachers but also from one's strength (and where does one get this strength?) to resist the rhetorically powerful.

Philosophical learning does not result in complete knowledge but rather in an original way of participating in an ongoing discussion. The flow of other words typical of discussion cannot be understood within the egological perspective still dominant in chapter 2. Holding a conversation means allowing the other person to speak *as* other from me. The other is not only there for me (as teacher, assistant, or discussion partner) but also, and first of all, for himself. Without the irreplaceable and irreducible contribution of the other's otherness, the conversation loses its philosophical relevance. It is different and cannot be replaced by the "internal dialogue" of a self-sufficient ego.

If perfect philosophers were possible, all conversations would have to culminate in the imperium of the whole truth: a Monologue would only formulate dogmas; the one and only true ideology would make perfect peace through universal indoctrination. Nations, Churches, and political parties have appealed to such truth to justify wars and camps for the extermination of falsehood. Are violence and rhetoric inevitable when people believe they "possess" the one, the whole, and the pure truth? No, if that truth has an infinite respect for all attempts at independent thinking, and no, if the "possessors" do not know they have the whole truth (in which case they would not possess the whole truth because something would be lacking in their knowledge). No, if they know that truth is unobtrusive, and act accordingly. If they think it is useless to reflect on other perspectives in the belief that the history of truth-seeking has reached its goal, then violence and rhetoric *are* inevitable. Can I take another speaker seriously if I am convinced of my "possessing" the truth? Or, is it essential for genuine thought to remain a never-ending search. modestly allowing other seekers to speak?

1. Philosophy as dialogue

Philosophizing is a reflective search for the one, unique, and total truth. This definition is not undone by insisting on the inevitability of thought's limited perspective. The definition of perspective necessarily contains a nonperspectivist moment incessantly propounded by the impulse that powers every serious and radical thought.

The conflict between our desire for the one and total truth and our imprisonment in a perspective limited by time, culture, education, and individuality makes our struggle for the Great Synthesis not impossible, but naive: an overseer and ruler of the universe acting as a god is actually a mere window through which certain things can be seen. Whoever understands this understands that neither his nor any other synthesis can be the final word. All syntheses are important as long as they have a certain level and quality. A thinker cannot give up his struggle for overviews because thinking *is* putting things together. Yet he sees his way of thinking as one of the many different possibilities. Since "the truth" cannot be my individual monopoly, I see in my "truth" *one* (possible) truth, whose value depends on the extent to which it partially realizes the necessary idea of the one, whole, and genuine truth. With this formulation I do not want to suggest that truth is an unattainable treasure independently existing somewhere (even if this image is not altogether untrue). The idea of a pure and complete truth rules all authentic thinking. The discoveries of thoughtful activity do not abolish, but rather enrich, its limited perspective. In spite of, *and thanks to*, the peculiarity of my individual limitation, I can put something into words that is worthwhile in its own right, and also for others. I think and try my "word" as a more or less successful attempt. Other attempts can and must also be tried out. On my journey I look ahead to different "words" — other contributions bearing shadows or reflections of the truth.

I cannot invent those other words. Of course I can think of alternatives, other methods, formulations, divisions, and arguments, but

I cannot defend them *as others*. Whenever I formulate them, they are steps in my own train of thought. They are, for example, suggestions I accept or objections I refute. They are submitted to the movement and style of my way; in being stolen from others, they change their individuality. The words I seek as complement and correction to my own must confront me with other approaches, must give expression to other thinkers *as others* and not as possible elements of a system in which I can recognize my own thoughts. I can speak in the name of others and explain what they mean, or reconstruct their answers to possible questions, but I can only do this after others have first spoken or written.

If every thought is partially determined by the *haecceitas* of a unique individual, no monologue can truly and concretely transcend its own perspective — although the very concept of a perspective refers our thought to something beyond itself. The only way of overcoming the boundaries of our strictly individual perspective is by receiving the words of others who are also thinking and speaking for the sake of truth. *The encounter with other thinkers is essential to the method of philosophy.*

By listening and reading, I discover that others think and have thoughts. This discovery precedes my own independent thought. In striving for a certain mastery, a pupil does not do away with authority. This is insufficiently maintained by a hermeneutics that integrates words into an enriched monologue. A master philosopher is not a conqueror, but a participant in a conversation of related minds in which each treats the other as an authority.

The attempt to overcome the monological structure of philosophy necessarily raises the question; How are all the words of others and of mine related to one another? What unity do their interconnected differences form? How must we describe the constellation of thinkers presenting themselves to one another in radically divergent words?

It is not that truth is merely the whole of all the represented standpoints and syntheses. For (a) it is not certain that all possible standpoints have been expressed (what is the criterion for determining possible standpoints?) and (b) it is not certain that the syntheses presented are sufficiently true to be important; an entire epoch and all philosophies within it can be untrue and inauthentic. Does the expression *all standpoints* really mean anything? Does the word *all* mean empirical endlessness or a universe that can be defined, for example in a superhuman monologue?

How we are to define and understand the constellation of existing (true and untrue) philosophies is a problem of the history of philosophy. The meaning of this constellation in our search for truth is one of the fundamental questions of systematic philosophy. The historical multiplicity of different philosophies form a togetherness that cannot be summarized by any individual. This togetherness is not a synthesis. Monologues that summarize remain necessary; they prove that searching really does go on; thus, radicality and coherence are sought. The same goes for hermeneutical appropriation and retrievals. However, every attempt at a synthesis is governed from the beginning by the norm requiring it to join a dialogue in which no one has the last word. In order to recognize the truth that no one is a god, to let others speak, and to respect the validity of all serious attempts at truth, my monologue must change into a fragment of the greater conversation of proposals and counterproposals, which can neither be overcome nor ended by any individual conclusion. Every attempt to transform this dialogue into a system of my own is a mere inauguration of another stage. There is no final word. There is no final time. There is no omniscient authority.

Based on the foregoing, it is now possible to formulate some of the conditions necessary for a fruitful dialogue.

Most important, I must permit other thinkers to speak *as others*. I am and remain only a participant. Modesty does not prevent me from seeking and defending my findings in my way, passionately opposing what I find to be inauthentic or untrue. A fierce struggle for truth is very different from a dictatorship.

Of all the thoughtful "words" that others have produced, the best deserve priority. They are so numerous that I must make choices. But even if I were able to study all of them, the question would remain: how will I recognize the "best," or in general, how do I recognize the quality of philosophical conceptions?

One criterion, which simultaneously establishes a kinship among interlocutors, is in the orientation of the expressed thought towards the truth itself. In this the speakers recognize their common inspiration. But how is this orientation ascertained?

Dialogue is the totality of the interactions through which a family of thinkers comes to be. How do their encounters develop?

An analysis of the conversation in which truth is at stake seems appropriate to attain more clarity about the structure and conditions of philosophy as an ongoing dialogue.

2. Conversations in search of truth

Not every conversation is relevant to an understanding of philosophy. If two or more people converse, intending to discover truth, their conversation realizes an intention from which philosophy derives its meaning. An analysis of such a conversation will therefore be illuminating for an understanding of (the essence of) philosophy.

Three elements of this conversation seem to be clear:

1. There are at least two speakers.
2. Their speaking requires exchange and time.
3. Their speaking aims at (more) truth.

The third element provides food for thought, to be discussed in the last chapter. The first two are analyzed in this section, and the following sections will relate them in a more concrete way to the problematic of this book.

2.1 *Speaking*

The participants in a conversation about truth are similar in many ways. Each is motivated by a desire for truth and experiences his and the others' speech as part of a search that must lead to further insight. Whether their conversation actually brings them closer to (the) truth is not certain, but that certainly is their intention. This intention is the norm of their conversation, from which certain conditions follow: a sincerity of intention and expression, the courage to go beyond the familiar, and the modesty to admit both that no one is a master of the universe and that "the truth" is too great for any of us. Other "virtues" necessary for the joint search may be deduced from the underlying aim of philosophy, which is to be neither sceptical nor dogmatic. These virtues comprise the "morality" belonging to an authentic search for truth. But the dialogical character of philosophy is thereby not yet revealed. The "morality" of thinking indicated here is applicable to all the participants, but it does not yet express their mutual relations. As it is derived from every participant's orientation towards truth (which is greater than any individual's speech *and* greater than that of all the speakers taken together), this morality rules their conversation, but as such it reveals neither the demands implied in their dialogue nor the nature of their togetherness. These cannot become clear, unless we pay attention to what constitutes the differences between the interlocutors. Equality in the search is a necessary condition for an affinity and a feeling of solidarity, but it does not constitute intersubjectivity. However, inequality is also essential.

Speaking is always speaking to *another*. "Thinking aloud" (and inner dialogues, as well) are directed at someone other than the speaker. They are ways of doubling oneself. Speaking always includes two persons: the person speaking and the person spoken to. Even as a conversation with myself, speaking is a *speaking to*; it does not make sense if I direct my inner words to no one, or if this other "I" is a mere illusion. Speech implies a particular kind of duality.

The person to whom I address myself is faced with the opposite otherness: he understands what I say as an activity inspired by a certain intention and pretension. By directing myself to the listener, I intrude on his living-ahead-of-himself, his thinking, musing, planning, and being silent. I claim to have something to say and force him to listen. Between invitation and coercion there are many gradations, but even the sweetest word is an attack on the other's privacy. It can be a pleasant surprise or a long-awaited answer. Nevertheless, it befalls the receiver as something beyond his control. If I hear a word directed at me, I do not and cannot produce it. Only another can pronounce it. If I take it up into my *cogito* and pronounce it anew, it is a quotation. It refers to the speaker I have heard. When I appropriate a word I have heard, I can eliminate its author by abstracting the speech's content. The traditional way in which Western philosophy has taken up, analyzed, and assimilated words and texts is a similar abstraction. Appropriation has taken place through transforming spoken and written words into the elements of new monologues. The others remained alive as long as the real, or possible, sense of their texts was taken up, but their otherness disappeared into the new texts to which this assimilation process gave birth.

The difference between speaker and listener, pointed out here in a very formal way, has a phenomenal concreteness. Some of its elements must now be described.

A conversation for the sake of truth has meaning only if something new is said, by one side at least. This "news value" is grounded in the surprising character of speech referred to above: it always appears as something unexpected. By his mouth and eyes, or — if I cannot see him — by his voice, intonation, and emotional force, the speaker comes upon me, creating and establishing something new. I cannot withdraw. I must choose either to deal with his words in my own way or to ignore them.

The "news" brought forth may be an expression of something I have already thought or suspected or vaguely felt. Still, what is said is different. This becomes evident, for example, when you express a thought that I have already entertained. It sounds different from the same thought in my "head" and provokes me to questions, doubts, criticism, and so on. I find myself more in opposition to it than when it was a moment in my own world and thought.

The news that you tell me can also be a clarification of my own thoughts or feelings, for example when you translate or interpret what I have said. You can urge me to explain or correct my thoughts by asking questions. You can open my eyes to unknown connections. Listening to the spoken word always involves an element of learning. The news is not necessarily good: the claims of another's speech can be destructive; nevertheless, they always represent a mastery to me, the listening party. In this sense, every act of listening is a learning and every act of speaking is an instruction. The intention of speech for the sake of truth includes (even if it does not pronounce genuine truths) the pretension of instruction. Every act of speaking is a claim to mastery.

If only one of the parties speaks (for example, in a lecture to which the audience reacts only through various kinds of applause or reproval), no conversation arises, even if the reaction can be understood as an agreement. If questions can be asked, an exchange may start. Critical questions are attempts at changing the balance of influence, but they still allow the speaker to maintain the central position. This is also the case in discussions in which one speaker dominates and acts as "master," while the other speakers are mere budding teachers. When the speakers are alternately master and pupil for each other, however, a discussion between "equals" arises. Their equality rests on the inequality that makes them both giver and receiver in turn. Both have something (new) to say, which, at least in a certain respect, the other cannot draw from himself.

A conversation in which nothing new is discussed can have meaning as a pause in the search for truth. It expresses little of the difficult trial and error that is typical of this search. Although speech that confirms what the listener already knows still brings something new, the newness of the other's words shows that a conversation cannot stop at a mutual affirmation of the same truth.

An objection arises here. Are form and content not confused by saying that a word spoken to another contains something new, just because of its otherness? Why should the content of that expression change if another, and not I, pronounces it?

The *phenomenon* of speaking is an occurrence of something new: it surprises the listener and has a certain strangeness, *even for the speaker.* He, too, is surprised by it. By stressing the difference between form and content, the objection tries to salvage the identity of the "word," in spite of the differences between the speaker and the listener. It maintains that the phenomenon of speaking can be explained within the familiar framework of a philosophy of the universal. This philosophy takes its stand beyond the individuality of individuals, summarizing their thinking and speaking in the form of "common" thoughts. The preceding discussion, however, has set out two lines of thought through which this presupposed universal may be challenged.

A first refutation begins with the assertion that a philosophical "word" (I use this expression here as a metaphor for a whole argument) is meaningful only within the context of other (philosophical, scientific, literary, etc.) related words. This context is part of its meaning. If it is true, as argued above, that the content and the meaning of all the words spoken by a philosopher are perspectivized, and that the ultimate perspective is constituted by the uniqueness of his individuality, then *the meaning of his words is also unique and strictly individual.* This interpretation corresponds more closely to the experience of speaking as a presentation of something new than to the explanation that denies the impossibility of a content's repetition. It also escapes the vulgar nominalism of meaning by simultaneously maintaining the possibility and reality of a thorough affinity between the thinkers, who also produce a concrete and nonreductive universality.

The second line of argumentation begins with the individuality of the speaker. Your speaking expresses a position by which the self engages itself. Along with your voice, melody, rhythm, and emotions, your thoughts are also your own. Ideas become disconnected from your individuality just as little as do your other attributes. The ability to communicate with others and achieve agreement by expressing your thoughts does not negate, but rather emphasizes, the uniqueness of those thoughts. The more individual they are, the more they have to say. The possibility of their validity being recognized by many, or even by all, does not invalidate their occurrence *only* in the form of unique thoughts, thought here and now by this speaker. Thoughts are not lifeless realities, existing independently from the consciousness of their thinkers. If the former thinking in which they existed is not transmitted by a later retaking, they disappear. Active thought produces words, letters, and texts; if another thinker does not bring them to life again, they remain mere possibilities. Pure universality, unsullied by individuality, "exists" only as a possibility. But what kind of "existence" does a possibility have? Being possible means precisely that: although it can, it does *not*, exist. Even if we admit one superindividual intellect that thinks and keeps universality alive, individual speakers are still its concrete and unique editions. Every word is strictly an individual expression. Every word is news. Not a single word is isolated, either from the speaker's context or from that exchange of words called a "discussion."

When something new is said to me, I am approached by something strange.If the spoken word contains a whole philosophy — and as a truth-seeking speaking, it always does in a more or less explicit way — great effort is demanded of me in working my way into the other's train of thought and context. The spoken word urges me to see, think, and feel *differently* than I do when I follow my own spontaneous inclinations. The estrangement I am invited to can be very difficult to accomplish, especially when the other comes from afar. I can disregard the claim in the spoken words; I can also make the words harmless by forcing them into my own language and framework so that they have nothing new to say. The act of listening, however, presupposes that I allow myself to be carried out from my own center. What I find to be self-evident is then suspended; by way of a test, I allow myself to be persuaded to assume another vision. I abandon my mind, at least provisionally, to the different logic, rules, and patterns of another way of thought. The other's speech turns me around.

Such a change does not eliminate the demand for autonomous thinking that is necessary for a philosopher. His temporary silence in reflecting on others' words remains motivated by the struggle to examine everything critically *himself* and, if possible, to retake it for his own. The path of critical receptivity runs between a total submission to the speaker and a relapse into a dogmatic monologue. The reaction demanded by the word can be schematized as follows.

Listening is a complying, thinking, enjoying, seeing, and feeling along with what is said; as a tentative agreeing, measuring, and exploring of its possibilities, it absorbs something strange. What is said demands my reflection and distant appropriation, as a kind of test: I examine its internal coherence within the speaker's context, his own principles, norms, and presuppositions. If I do this thoroughly, I reconstruct the entire constellation of the other's speech.

The testing, however, also occurs from an external point of view. The distance between the speaker and me makes it impossible for me to deny my own framework, context, and system. I must assert them, in spite of my willingness to let the other speak. I do not maintain my conviction as though I had the patent on truth or as though my criteria were absolutely unassailable, but rather to create a tension between two "words," my own and the other's, that struggle with each other in various degrees.

This awakened tension forces me to examine both my own and the other's speaking, thinking, and experience. Another's speech causes a double distance in me: distance to what is said and distance from my own presuppositions and criteria, robbed of their self-evidence and security. I do not give them up, but I allow them to be discussed. I go into a state of not "knowing for sure": an undecidedness that must be decided, a crisis that becomes more critical, as the other examines things more thoroughly. The confrontation with a living other tries the listener's own strength. When a word shocks, it uproots the recipient. As listener, I sometimes have more difficulty with my own convictions than with providing an answer to the speaker. If his speech is very fundamental, there are no ready criteria or methodological rules for solving the crisis it generates. The radicality of another's word makes the hitherto accepted rules questionable.

Such a crisis can be beneficial, namely, when it results in a reordering of life, thought, vision, and feeling, making them more fruitful and true than was the old order of truth. Perhaps this is even necessary for a thorough renewal. For where will we find the newness that shocks our familiar framework, except in the word that is truly other? Reflection, meditation, and prayer can also undermine worn-out habits and dogmas and renew a person — but is such a renewal not experienced as the fruit of an (inner) word as well, one that breezes by, rustles, separates, connects, or creates?

A parenthetical remark

Even by no longer putting its faith in the monologue but by expecting truth from good conversation, philosophy still does not eliminate the struggle towards system and synthesis. The words that compose a truth-oriented conversation receive their value from the degree to which they offer insight. An insight, however, is not an isolated statement, because it involves an overview and context as wide as the civilization of which such words and views are expressions. A struggle for coherence, broad horizons, and synthesis is essential to *every* search for truth — both philosophical and "spiritual." The burden of finding and building, on one's own, cannot be avoided by "talking things over" together. Dialogue is not a refuge for exhausted souls who lack the strength to deepen and stretch their thoughts into the dimensions of a system. Systematizing, stamina, and a courageous bid for the widest and most radical are essential for genuine and profound thoughts and lives. Although every system represents only a particular whole, and thus only one perspective and vision, the quality of a dialogue depends on the synthetic force of the designs in it. A conversation owes its thoroughness to the radicality and breadth of scope expressed in the words composing it. A good conversation does not replace systems but sets them into a specific relationship with one another. The speakers are responsible for the quality of their arguments. The coherence resulting from the syntheses of their encounters with one another is not a highest synthesis or supersystem, but rather a unique form of (meta)philosophy.

2.2 *Dialogue*

As speaker, I am successful when my words elicit a response. Total silence or applause interrupts or ends my speaking. The listener who assimilates what I have said can produce an answer, which can stimulate me in return. My listener becomes speaker and vice versa. Master and pupil exchange places.

The difference between speaker and listener does not exclude a certain unanimity; in fact, it demands it. The consensus presupposed by every conversation has certain characteristics of *form* and *content*.

1. The *formal conditions* for a conversation directed towards truth are the following:

To speak with one another means that all forms of destruction are excluded. Murder, suppression, censorship, excommunication, ridicule, contempt, and the like destroy speech before it is spoken, even if the speaker who uses such methods on his "opponent" manages to say whatever he wants to say. Yet struggle and polemic, even hate, do not make a conversation impossible. Every conversation may even be seen as a "fight" as will be shown. But if it is not to degenerate into pure barbarism, a fight must be accompanied by a profound unanimity.

This can be illustrated by the "method" of fighting. Like every conversation, a verbal fight follows certain rules and has its own (methodo)logic. The whole of logic can perhaps be developed from the idea of dialogue and its necessary conditions. Whenever interlocutors argue, each of them assumes that they agree on the meaning and nature of acceptable ways of arguing — at least for the most part. If I want to show the other something, I refer to experiences that I assume the other may also have had. Our conversation may also deal explicitly with the presuppositions of (other) conversations without thematizing them. For example, thoughts may be exchanged about the nature and structure of an argument, about definitions, about the importance of experiences, and so on. This sort of "metaconversation" again has its own implicit presuppositions and agreements. The questioning of the presuppositions on which "speaking together" rests cannot, however, be repeated without end. There must either be a starting point that cannot be questioned any further, or we must stop our questioning with an arbitrary decision.

The idea of conversation implies a fundamental consensus, only possible if both speakers

a. speak *and*
b. listen;
c. aim at truth;
d. understand each other's language;
e. understand each other's way of thinking;
f. do not live in two worlds whose *contents* totally differ (see 2 below).

The essential moments and conditions of (a) speaking and (b) listening have been discussed above (in section 2.1). The intention to search for truth (c) is discussed in chapter 4. An analysis of (d), the common language, implies the difficult question of the extent to which dead languages can be translated into living ones, one living language into another, technical languages into everyday language, one system into another, and so on. In considering (e), the unity and the differences of various ways of thinking, we cannot avoid discussing the unity and differences of (onto- and methodo-)logics nor asking if an all-encompassing logic, a final super- or metalogic, is possible.

2. The *conditions governing the content* of a conversation are not completely independent of the formal conditions (especially of understanding each other's language) that allow speakers to understand one another. They refer to cultural "prejudices" usually considered to be self-evident truths, which the interlocutors are unaware of as prejudices. To eliminate them one can play other prejudices off against them, modify them, or even disjoint them in a creative way. The intention to pursue truth that is characteristic of philosophical conversations forbids our uncritical surrender to the prejudices and traditions we have inherited, but it does not provide a creative starting point, or super standpoint, outside the culture that has taught us to speak. The coincidence of an intention-for-truth with culture-boundness makes for the *critical* character of all truth-seeking speech. A philosophical conversation examines the words it produces: every repetition of familiar sayings is questioned; every newly risked expression must defend itself against old and new contradictions.

The newness of every instance of speech implies that inter-locutors do not only agree but also disagree with one another, at least in the sense of not-yet-agreeing. If they agree in everything, their exchange of words is no longer a search for truth but a joint enjoy-ment, a repose in the common conviction of an attained truth. This is philosophical paradise.

Because a genuine conversation is also characterized by dis-agreement, epigones do not truly contribute to philosophical conver-sations; they merely refer back to the great masters who have something to say. The latter must remain partners in our con-versations. However, epigones may not be their best mouthpieces. Commentaries by disciples may elucidate their master's text, but in their dependence, their thinking capacity is obviously not great enough to encompass their master's truth. As partners and guides epigones can be useful, but true philosophy requires that a thinker measure himself against the great texts, which speak for themselves.

2.3 *Topics of conversation*

The unity of consensus and difference in a truth-oriented con-versation expresses itself in the topic discussed. What is life? Does pain have a meaning? How can we understand vegetative excess? What does a diagnosis of our time reveal? Such questions keep our dialogues alive.

During verbal exchanges, particularly when they fall into repe-titions and harsher tones, speakers may discover that unthematized presuppositions and "self-evident propositions" are what is causing the impasse in their dialogue. Such impasses may lie in the content, but they may also consist of the various viewpoints, methods, and logics governing the interlocutors' thinking. In the later case a fruit-ful conversation is not possible, unless the participants pay attention to these formal elements, treating them as explicit themes of a joint examination.

The discovery and explicit discussion of deeply hidden pre-logical, emotional, or spiritual *a prioris* are even more difficult. Even logics do not always immediately grasp these, but they nonetheless penetrate and direct every act of speaking, as psychoanalysis, socio-logy, and psychology have shown.

In content, logic, and the prelogical we can distinguish various levels between surface and depth. There are thus many possibilities of discussing, of profound questioning, of seeking a deeper unit, or of retreating in the face of painful discoveries and refraining from proceeding further, beyond what one is accustomed to.

Criticisms of currently held opinions and "democratically ascertained" decisions or institutions, the undermining of common-sense convictions, the discovery of psychological, sociological, and historical conditions responsible for our accepting as self-evident what other spirits, times, and cultures did not believe, analyses of the unconscious and suppressed desires motivating our thinking and speaking, analyses of the language reflexes that have deceived us: all of these and more in the realm of self-criticism are necessary in order to make speaking more honest, freer, and more compatible with its goal. If speakers differ but little, they hardly provoke one another to self-criticism and conversions. Since the most radical provocation comes from truth itself (see chapter 4), their discussion *can* bring them further, but they fall short of the turnabout that fundamental differences may compel. The deeper the difference, the more one *can* learn from it. But speakers often abandon their argument prematurely. Perseverance is indeed very difficult. To realize this, speakers must genuinely search for truth, allow criticism, question others as well as themselves, and have enough strength to let go of their own conviction, at least provisionally. The progress and regress demanded of them is not a purely theoretical activity. Since thinking is rooted in a vital, emotional, and practical ground that precedes any distinction between the theoretical and practical, a (self)critical speaking demands, and occasions, radical changes and profound reversals.

The ideal of every thorough conversation is a communion of all the participants in the pure, and whole, truth. But, this remains unattainable. All speech particularizes thought. Even if silence and singing increase when the chatter of fashion, the media, and science are overcome, the triumph of a harmonious chorus remains a distant prospect. The envisioning of this Utopia is productive, however, because it lengthens and improves the endless conversation of those who seek for truth.

2.4 *Conversation, combat, violence (or: dialogue and rhetoric)*

2.4.1 SPEAKING AS FIGHTING

Every conversation is a fight.[11]

The teaching and listening of master and pupil precedes the dialogue of equals. However, as we have also seen, every act of speaking exercises a certain mastery when it has something (new) to say. In this sense, speaking is essentially authoritative. An offering of the "word" is always the self-presentation of an authority. It demands to be heard; it is obtrusive; it forces one to listen and provokes a response.

Words have *power*. They hit, wound, slash, silence, kill. Even the friendliest of words ("Listen . . . "; "Shall we discuss this calmly . . ."; "I think you're nice . . . ") are ways of persuading another to go in the speaker's direction. The power of words, the authority of their expression, does not coincide with their content. There is a surplus, a power, that has effects beyond what is understood in the words.

Since the repartee provoked by the speaker expresses the listener's own stance, every reply is to some extent a contradiction. No conversation escapes the conflict that begins a struggle. Every dialogue is thus simultaneously a *discussion*, and every discussion, aside from being a search for community, is also a competition among colleagues who disagree with one another because they are aiming at the same thing.

If violence may be defined as an exercise of power that causes others to do certain deeds or to hold opinions that they would not do or hold on their own initiative, we must say that every speech is, more or less, violent. This same definition of violence, however, also forces us to say that anyone who follows his own motivations without understanding them is violently propelled.

Unclear desires and drives are a violence from within. I cannot do away with this violence by freely choosing where my own inclinations are to lead. It happens — in fact it is common — that I often choose to follow the various expressions of a dark *pathos*. It is not possible to eliminate all violence! We would have to extinguish all affectivity and all speech. The question, then, is not how we can eliminate all violence, but rather, as Aristotle asked in his exemplary way, how the unavoidable violence of drives and struggle can be purified and changed into goals and intentions of "the spirit," that is, of reason and civilization. In terms of the conditions governing a truth-oriented conversation, this means that it is a waste of effort, unworthy of attempt, to eliminate all compulsion and struggle from speaking. What matters is the refining of verbal competition so that it can become (more) civilized and (more) human — an ethics of discussion, a good dispute.[12]

The highest norm for the ethics sought here lies in the power of truth itself. Both the compulsion necessarily exercised by every speaker and the resistance of his opponent's reply have a positive value, as long as their fight and "violence" fight against another violence: that of the destructive or distorting forces coming from fraudulent, irrational, and barbarous methods and motives.

2.4.2 RHETORIC

We now come to the problem of rhetoric. When a speaker, especially a truth-seeking speaker, gives force to his words by other than rational means (e.g., by being preachy or by taking advantage of the vogue), a critique is necessary — not only of his way of speaking but also of his content.

Not all rhetoric is evil, however. The power play resulting from emotional energy, from the inevitable authority of human speech and its surplus of force, can be subordinated to the power of truth.

Since truth is not a purely theoretical but an existential concern as well, it must be *conquered*. *Abstract* thought is not adequate to this end. Having truth as his ideal mobilizes the entire life of a truth-loving individual. It governs and sets norms for his life's experiments. The philosopher's actions (elucidated by his thoughts) as well as his heart, the emotional source of his thoughts and projects, is wrapped up in his search for truth. If a human being reaches the point where he can speak the truth, he experiences a kind of liberation. Speaking the truth, then, is not merely a quiet affirmation but also an explosion of emotional energy — a rejoicing, even a singing. This sort of thinking is not far removed from poetry.

Searching for the truth is not yet a rejoicing, but rather an intensification of the entire person: a concentration of attention and drive that expresses itself even physically. The intensification of psychic energy caused by a passion for truth is accompanied by a relaxation, a release from things that do not matter. It would be unjust, however, to divide these sides between spirit and corporeality. Seeking the truth comes from something that is simultaneously more fundamental and more material than thinking. Thinking is the expression of a deep-seated passion that awakens and drives it. Although the kind of thinking a philosopher desires generates and explains itself, human existence — its affectivity and corporeality — cannot be understood as the externalization of an Idea justifying itself by its self-knowledge. According to absolute Idealism, the Idea learns nothing new by going outside itself into the psyches and bodies of individual people, but the spiritualistic schema (built on a logically preceding dualism) reduces all rhetoric to a shell without any truth of its own. It sees in all incomprehensible elements only a metaphor, one that ought to be translated into theory. It denies every surplus beyond understanding. According to this conception, even the *language* of understanding is nothing other than an (unimportant, even false, because it is time-consuming) expression of the eternal truth, existing only in the actual comprehension of the Concept. If understanding is not itself the source but is rather an exponent of one's deepest desires, a rhetorical way of speaking, just like a poetic one, may contain a peculiar moment of truth that cannot be translated into comprehensibility. The experience of philosophizing confirms this idea: thought and understanding are guided by a deep-rooted affectivity.

2.4.3 POLEMIC

If the foregoing is correct, we can understand why speaking or writing is a sort of wrestling. It forces its way in spite of all theoretical and external resistance. The denial of certain other thoughts may demand social courage, but the fight against one's own untruthfulness demands even greater strength.

Truthfulness, as a condition for the search, is a pretheoretical, practical, and emotional condition for good theory. Fighting untruthfulness is an essential part of the philosophical search. This is, therefore, a battle: within the perspective of truth, speaking necessarily becomes *polemic*. It remains so as long as it crosses the social and individual dimensions of what is not genuine. Criticism is an essential element of all philosophy, but it is a mistake to limit it to theoretical analysis. Truth also demands correction of the dispositions preceding theory.

The power of pretheoretical untruthfulness resists rational insights as well as all forms of truth. If one's speaking is really concerned with truth, it fights against the violence of that power. It is therefore necessarily militant, aggressive, and in a certain sense, violent.

The vehemence of rhetorical speaking can arise from the feeling that someone will not be convinced by rational arguments because he is not concerned with (the) truth. This "someone" is not necessarily another; the cause of my vehemence can also be within me — my own youth, my lack of daring to be what I am, or my own concealed lies. Insofar as nontheoretical factors prevent my secure possession of the truth, the polemic is essential to a serious search for truth. An absence of verbal battles is a symptom of indifference and *not* necessarily of "good manners."

However, not every polemic is a manifestation of love for the truth. Vehemence in speaking can also betray jealousy, resentment, bitterness, and forms of dishonesty. The conditions for a good polemic can be deduced from the intention peculiar to truth-oriented discussions.

If we look at the content of a discussion, we see the following. Supposing that (1) all the interlocutors are aiming at truth, (2) their speaking approaches (the) truth, at least to some degree, and (3) they do not break their conversation; their expressed differences are instructive. The more radical they are, the more they can learn and the greater the chance that their individual speaking will become more thorough by taking the measure of those differences. Much courage and patience are necessary for such an encounter. It would be best to seek out those who are most distant from one's own ideas, those who are at the utter opposite end of the spectrum, for discussion. This *Fernstenliebe* — love for the "farthest" — demands that one resist every inclination to ridicule or belittle another and instead convert such negativity into recognition and respect for his otherness.

A great thought does not easily accept subjugation. Since it is great, it anticipates and refutes much criticism; its foundations are resistant to undermining. The impregnability of a great philosophy is a sign of its strength, but this attribute also makes it vulnerable. Indeed, the *basis* of such a philosophy, whose questions have yet to be answered by the criticized philosopher, can be made into the object of critical reflection. The discussion of starting points that arises can make history, if it is done in great style. Assuming that all the participants are driven by a desire for truth, there is no reason for vehement polemics, and even less of one for a fight in the name of truth.

Vehemence is less unsuitable in connection with faults of a more formal nature. For example, when someone is ignorant or does not know of certain problems and yet claims expertise in the subject, irritation and angry reactions can result. Any irrational behavior leading to aggression betrays the orientation to (more) truth. An attitude that is unwilling to accept the truth rightly awakens indignation, as do superficiality and insincerity. Do they give one the right to react sharply, with spiritual slaughter or superior irony, for example?

A quiet answer or a simple repetition of what has been said *can* be a devastating criticism. Its acceptance requires the listener or reader to understand it as criticism and to be ready to prefer truth over falsity. The question, however, is: is he prepared to do this? Is he so enamored of the truth that he is willing to back down himself, if necessary?

There are many forms of untruthfulness: swearing by a revered teacher or by the dogmas of an institution, party, or school; fear of not being in style; lack of courage in facing practical consequences; impurity; a desire for acceptance; and so on. On this terrain, too, every vice demands an appropriate reaction. The general question is whether, and under what circumstances, these reactions may utilize a certain rhetorical "violence."

2.4.4 AN ETHICS OF VIOLENCE

The question of the legitimate use of rhetorical violence is part of the problem of compulsion within the framework of *education* and *politics*. The classical justification for a certain violence sees it as *counter*violence, necessitated by a preceding "primary" violence that disturbs the rational foundations of a human society. A murderer forces the state to check his violence. From his behavior he is obviously not open to reason, since reason demands, as a necessary condition for society, that members of a society not destroy one another. Society must, then, make the murderer harmless through means that, if taken in isolation, are unreasonable and, in that sense, violent. The justification simultaneously indicates *how far* this counterviolence may go: it is completely subordinate to its goal (society, as such) and may not go further than is necessary to prevent primary violence or to rectify the damage done. The norm given with this justification, therefore, also contains a restriction.

The same principle applies to the philosophies of education and self-education, or self-development. Compulsion may be necessary in order to counter irrational behavior. If the voice of reason is not heeded, a child's behavior can be harmful to himself and to others. Such behavior must be controlled to whatever extent is necessary for preventing or correcting the harm. The same is true for a person seeking guidelines for self-development through reason. The lowest degree of self-knowledge discerns irrational impulses and tendencies — immoderate "passions." Ennobling them requires a long history of fighting their inclination to absolutize themselves. Reason mobilizes other forces against the unreasonable violence of the impulses — not to eliminate the spontaneous dynamic of the "passions," but rather to maintain their energy for more civilized work. We must give to the confusion of feelings a human form, and channel natural energies into a more genuine humanness. The process runs according to periods, which can perhaps be characterized in the following way.

A new period begins when I discover that my life is being ruled by hidden emotions (e.g., desire, fear, or despondency) that I can no longer tolerate. This discovery occasions a crisis in my life. A certain disintegration threatens. I know I must begin again. Rational deliberation is necessary, but not enough. I also need an ideal image to help me inaugurate a better attitude and better behavior. Such an image is partly derived from other, exemplary lives, partly from an individual projection of better possibilities for myself. Inspired by an idealized self-image, I try to fashion my behavior according to it. To this end I must bend certain tendencies or subordinate them to other tendencies. Thus, I engage in a play of forces, in a wrestling. The impulse driving everything must not be wasted or destroyed; it must be mobilized towards overcoming the chaos that would arise if I left my spontaneous drives to themselves. The violence perpetrated in a genuine form of self-development humanizes destructive forces by disciplining them. Therefore, civilization and rationality also have an aspect of subjugation, insofar as they prevent our passions to become wild and chaotic. This aspect is, of course, only one moment of a true integration.

The theory of self-development, education, and politics given above justifies a certain perpetration of violence, under the following conditions:

1. Justifiable violence presupposes a preceding violence that cannot be dealt with through nonviolent means;

2. The goal of this *second* violence, this *anti*violence, limits it: the force exerted must be proportionate to the desired effect (prevention or rectification).

The opposition of *reason* and *passions* (or natural inclinations, emotional energy, etc.), an opposition typical of Greek-Western ethics, has perhaps had its day. If one interprets reason in a very formal sense, in which reasonable affectivity differs from a chaotic, spontaneous, or "natural" affectivity only through its structure (orientation, coherence, style), the difficulty of transition to a nondualistic conception of morality is probably minimal. I would, however, prefer to develop an ethics on the basis of fundamental moods and central affects that are propelled by the most profound desire. The interplay of forces of less central feelings in human life can be interpreted as the concrete expression of the "heart." The need to form and order our feelings and behavior, in view of our most genuine desire(s), necessitates the forceful action of the educator, the politician, and man in general. Against our tyrannical tendencies (for which not only our belly and underbelly but also our hearts and minds — e.g., reason's arrogance — are responsible), desire rebels through the affective violence of a very radical and, therefore, very subtle nature. The heart of the "antiviolence theory" can be taken up in a philosophy of feelings, which replaces the schema of reason and sensibility by considering levels and differences of affectivity.

2.4.5 CONDITIONS FOR A GOOD POLEMIC

If we reserve the word *polemic* for a coercive, energetic, rhetorically violent form of speaking and apply the classical apology for a certain degree of violence to it, it follows that the only polemics we can consider good are those that are provoked by unreasonable emotions (untruthfulness, bad intentions, egotism, etc.) and that maintain a proper measure in their vehemence. In the ethics of polemics, the question of pro or con becomes the question of the *degree* to which rhetorical violence is an adequate answer to the previously spoken word. In what name is one fighting here? Is it necessary to proceed in this way? Is it efficient?

Polemical speaking is a variation on the forceful confrontation occurring in *every* act of speech. The nonargumentative elements are more clearly perceptible in a polemic than in a peaceful conversation, although no discussion is ever made up of completely transparent reasons and theory. Fighting — a show of strength — results from the interlocutors' *differences*. The necessity to fight, however, can change into a virtue. Speaking also aims at the "sublimation" of aggression. The complete elimination of aggression would not only be a waste of incredible energy but would also destroy the speaker's individuality. Heroism, honor, holy war, patriotism, martyrdom, and other ideals have accepted violence in a noble manner. The manner of their fighting has been regulated by codes. A similar regulation is necessary for the violence of speech.

The rejection of rhetoric by philosophers ever since Plato stems from their opinion that truth is simply a question of seeing, "giving reasons," and having insight. Speakers, then, are mere pronouncers of the unimpassioned game of thought played by the concepts themselves. But if every speaker contributes an individual and irreplaceable moment of truth, the truth comes by means of a universal *war* — the father of all statements worthy of reflection. All against all, but in a civilized way — that is, in the service of truth. An ethics of polemics is not an apology for unimpassioned rationalizing, but rather a stylizing moderation of rhetorical violence. The medieval *Questiones disputatae* had their code of honor. The idea of the tournament corresponds to the necessity of the argument, in which the participants passionately argue against the enemies of truth.

Who can claim to be a lover of truth and not an enemy? Someone's difference of opinion with me was not mentioned above as a justified motive for a polemic; nor was the falsity of his statements. The polemic was motivated by some form of untruthfulness. The other rebels against the essence of truth itself and against the possibility of embracing it. He does not love the truth. But when can I say I am moved by respect, desire, and love for truth? Who is truthful and knows it?

The application of the ethical principles of polemics faces objections similar to those facing the classical defense of violence in politics and education. How can a politician be sure that the defense of "law and order" is indeed motivated by respect for human rights and freedom? Is an "anarchist" totally wrong in declaring his actions to be a counterviolence against institutionalized injustice? Even if the abstract theory of primary violence and counterviolence is correct, who can say (1) who began it and (2) if violence was committed? The same questions arise in education. What the educator deems unjust and irrational is sometimes experienced by the child as completely innocent and good. How do educators know they are right? Is it not possible that they themselves are led by secretly violent motives — for example, by the pleasure of ruling and giving orders? Such education will then work in a destructive fashion, and the pupils are right to rebel. Even someone who fights against the violence within himself can be mistaken. Even a little psychoanalysis can show that people's vehemence in turning against themselves may come from murky sources. Masochism, fear, self-hatred, and narcissism rule many ascetics, whose consciousness is full of morality. Self-discipline is not enough.

Fulmination against forms of untruthfulness, too, can have spurious motives. The arrogance couched in a certain vehemence is dangerous. Can the speaker endure the comparison of his pretension with the actual motives of his speaking? Fleeing into a relativism of truth that makes all claims impossible is forbidden by truth itself. But, is it not safer to abstain from all presumption and to speak in a manner totally devoid of passion? This shows more modesty than does an ostentatious indignation. It seems possible to withdraw from the fight in order to concentrate on the positive statements of truth. But no matter how affirmatively one works at it, arguments, and the refutation of opposed opinions, remain necessary in philosophy. When such opinions result from untruthfulness, the proper attitude is polemical.

If it is not possible to participate in the discussion of truth and to abstain from all polemics simultaneously, if fighting is an unavoidable element of intersubjectivity,[13] then it is essential for speakers to purify themselves from untruthfulness as much as possible. Polemic demands self-discipline, asceticism, practice in truthfulness, and the eventual genuineness of those who attempt it.

But there are dangers here, too. So many forms of self-discipline conceal narcissism. What someone believes to be a genuine love for truth can be moralism or fear, lack of imagination, unrecognized desire, sceptical arrogance, a slavish spirit. Aside from self-examination and meditation, a profound turn towards the true, which can be neither externally nor "objectively" ascertained by inner observation, is demanded. Even though a person may be led by a deep consciousness, the crepuscular domain accompanying all self-consciousness will suggest doubts about his own genuineness.

As a speaker, I experience the greatest self-criticism by exposing myself to another who listens and speaks to me. While what he presents can be untrue or unimportant, the fact that he listens and speaks to me is the greatest test that I undergo. In face of the other, I hear my own words differently. They reveal more than their actual intention. I am overcome by shame, as questionable motives become audible to me, even if the other does not notice them. Sometimes it is enough that another repeats my words, to make me aware of their weakness or insincerity. Even pure truths take on a vulnerable character when they are stated in the presence of another — they sound like a question: will the other, must the other, endorse these statements? Are they not disputable, or at least questionable? These questions refer to the content of my words and to their inspiration as well. My knowledge and my attitude towards the truth and towards my own (un)truthfulness are put to the test by the existence of the other.[14].

When the other speaks to me (even in a polemical way), I see him in the light of his, and my own, truthfulness. If his intention is not pure, his words sound false. It is possible that I hear in them a reflection of my own mixture of purity and impurity. If his speech is genuine, I enjoy it, even if it occasionally embarrasses me.

A great deal has been written about the therapeutic significance of dialogue, but perhaps not enough on the truth of the further speaking it prepares, and certainly not enough on the significance that the other's speaking has for the essence of philosophy.

2.4.6 UNIVERSAL POLEMICS?

A certain theoretical violence may and must be used when certain irrational forces arise against the attainment of (more) truth. On the other hand, much aggression is due to vanity, hurt pride, imperialism, and other vices.

One theory widely held in our time, however, goes further. It does not see rhetorical violence as an essential element of speaking nor, particularly, of speech claiming to present (the) truth. According to this theory, aggression expresses not a coincidental desire to subjugate others but a fundamental will to power that rules every human being. Will to power is the essence of being human. Every human being is a dangerous, murderous animal. Just as behavior cannot be other than violent, speaking is necessarily polemical. If I try to avoid all verbal violence in speaking or writing — for example, if I am impressed (oppressed!) by the Western reverence for unimpassioned rationality — then I repress my will to power. A careful analysis will bring the hidden aggression in every text and every speech to the fore and reveal its strategic structures. All texts are strategies. War is the father of all speech.

"Truth" would seem to be a strange expression in this context. The struggle inherent in every discussion is waged in view of power, that is, as an exercise of forces trying to outdo one another. The perspective here is force and strength, health and sickness, life and death. Nonetheless, it is not impossible to speak of truth, even in this context. However, there must be a relation between (more) truth and (greater) strength. If truth and energy are related, will to power and love of truth can converge, and perhaps even coincide. Truth-oriented speaking makes way for itself in a field of forces that constitute war. Strategy and polemics are essential elements of a true methodology.

If truth and force are *not* related, the question arises, which norms govern our conversations? Does the criterion for the quality of discussion consist only of the greatest forces as such? The greatest efficiency? Efficiency to what end? Or, can we no longer ask that? If there is no longer any criterion for qualifying a certain power as good or bad, the "right" of the mightiest triumphs. Power to the sophists! Away with Plato, who sought a more beautiful, true and better reality because he could not be satisfied with the brutality of the strongest forces in the polis and in the soul.

Let us hope that truth and power are not indifferent to each other. The theoretical culture that the West has been building since Parmenides and Heraclitus has humanized the power play of speech and writing into a strategic field in which the true and the good are central. In spite of the illusions and self-deceptions that Theory has brought upon itself as a polemic against sophism, the law of truth will not be given up before our civilization is exhausted. The humanization of the truth war does, however, demand an organization of its rhetorical elements, by which squabbling is changed into argumentative sport. The stipulations of the medieval *disputatio* were such an attempt at joining the trial of strength with the true search for truth.

2.4.7 DEMOCRATIC DELIBERATION

The organization of a truth-oriented conversation must not be confused by the misconception that everyone has an equal right to speak and that the best results can be expected from "democratic" deliberation. According to this view, it will be good and sufficient if everyone speaks his thoughts; the reasons each participant gives will be either strong enough or weak enough to obtain or lose the vote of the majority. Speaking and voting will not only result in the best solution for this group but also in the most correct ideas.

The presupposition of any democratic search for truth is weak. It assumes that the actuality of several (and ideally all) opinions can constitute the truth. In a pure relativism concerning truth, there is perhaps no other choice — except between silence and "democratic" voting procedures. In the latter case "truth" means an opinion agreed on by the majority, to which they subjugate all others (with or without permission).

The devil's advocate may call this representation a mere caricature. It does not take into account that the required deliberation must also involve the formulation and examination of arguments, and not merely the making of claims. This demand must indeed be recognized, as must the necessity of deliberating with others. But who urges these demands, and how are they realized?

There are sometimes participants in a discussion who do not understand what the others are saying. They sometimes do not even fully realize what they themselves are saying. Some do know what they are saying, but they do not provide arguments for it. Others give arguments, but their arguments are invalid. Are all these speakers to be corrected by some of the others, all of the others, a majority? The majority supposedly decides whether sensible opinions and decisive arguments have been given. This decision is made by a vote, that is, by nonargumentative procedure. Why should a majority be more capable of judging than an individual? In practical life, science, and philosophy, many "self-evident truths," universally recognized for long periods of time, have not withstood a closer examination of their claims to truth. If the majority were always right, it would be impossible to investigate its "truths" critically. Why should an individual be wrong if the majority does not understand or ignores his arguments — for example, when they are uncomfortable or difficult?

The description of nonrational motives behind our speaking is also applicable to joint deliberation. Here too, ulterior motives, insensitivity, partisan loyalty, vanity, and lack of genuineness play a role. The majority is not pure. While the critique, as an essential moment of another's speaking to me, *can* purify my convictions, this possibility is lost when the truth perspective becomes a question of *Who wins?* Only the truth itself decides; the majority has absolutely no right to claim a better insight than an individual's. The truth-seeking discussion is not an unqualified deliberation that results in one collective opinion; it is a continuous dialogue among speakers who are letting themselves be judged, not only by other speakers but primarily by truth itself.

If questions of truth are decided democratically, it is pure luck if the outcome is indeed true. One usually expects a compromise between the not-completely-true and the not-completely-untrue, at least if one believes that most people are somewhere between truthfulness and untruthfulness. There is, however, another special difficulty. Deliberation on truth is an argumentative, self-reflective speaking about difficult questions, and the nature of the questions and the manner of speaking involved require suitable skills from speakers and listeners. Not everyone is able to form a reasonable opinion on all questions. The short explanation and the concentrated evidence allowed by a limited discussion do not permit a thorough examination of complicated matters. How long one has to have worked in mathematics, chemistry, psychology, or exegesis before one is qualified to pass a proper judgment on the value of an idea or an argument! The subjects discussed in democracies are often philosophical in nature. The history of philosophy shows how difficult it is to understand them. The ease with which unqualified people judge is manifested in many cases of decision-making these days. Here the question does not concern which decisions a group must make regarding its own organization and action. Although making them implies certain unproven presuppositions in relation to the truth (of society, well-being, right, etc.), the decision cannot always be postponed. The group must do what it can and deserves the results of its efforts (even if some or most of its members suffer from them). However, when this procedure is held up as an example to a philosopher, he can only feel contempt for the naiveté of incapable people who make the final decisions on difficult questions — of which he has learned with difficulty how complicated they are.

The form or manner of speaking needed in joint deliberation — the art of argumentative conversations — demands a capacity acquired only by talent and practice. This is already the case at the level of reasoning and of the refined analyses provided by logic. It is even more so in a thoughtful speaking resulting from long experience in perceiving and meditation.

Despite these objections to a democratic search for truth, it seems difficult to propose an alternative. The idea of equal right in expressing one's own opinion is a protest against dogmas and ideologies imposing their domination under the guise of "truth." "Domination-free communication" (*herrschaftsfreie Kommunikation*) is necessary in countering the rhetorical violence of those claiming a special competence in correct speaking. How can such communication be organized, except as a forum where everyone can participate under the same conditions?

The absence of inequality in power is not enough, because it does not guarantee equality in intelligence, experience, or verbal, scientific, and philosophical ability. Whoever thinks that all of these inequalities are *effects* of domination is naive. Many indications make this hypothesis extremely implausible. Its defenders must make sure that unwillingness or a lack of genuineness does not disturb nonviolent discussion. Are these also the effects of violence? How then can violence itself ever come to be? Or, is violence itself the Principle of the only true cosmogony?

The conversation of serious truth-seekers is indeed a kind of forum, with no other authority except the truth itself. Whether those who truly have something to say are accepted as authorities depends on the quality of the participants. There is no formula for the production of truth, except in each interlocutor's honest and thoughtful speaking. The vehemence of the prophet does not contradict this. His verbal violence is sometimes beneficial as a protection against the imperialism of kings and masses. However, in the hope that certain unpolemical words will be accepted, now or later, because of their intrinsic strength, one can choose the greatest possible non-violence — and this can be beneficial, too. A universal abolition of testing strength is impossible. Even silence is not powerless; it touches both king and sophist, forcing each to answer. Every conversation is a force field. One must be strong in order to strengthen the position of truth.

2.4.8 POLEMICS AND RHETORIC

So far, rhetoric has been discussed only in the form of rhetorical violence. There is a strong tendency to identify the two. However, rhetoric involves more — evocation, suggestion, invention, and everything that gives speaking its emotional tone and depth, for example. The identification of rhetoric with verbal violence is probably still influenced by the traditional schema of Western thought referring to anything not "rational" (i.e., translatable into conceptual language) as violent. According to this schema, all feelings, inclinations, and passions are irrational forms of violence, insofar as they cannot be transformed into comprehensibility.

Some contemporary defenders of rhetoric deny this last point but maintain the solid opposition of conceptuality and violence (or power). But is there not a great deal of feeling in the world that can neither be conceptualized nor categorized as violence? Of course one can define "violence" so broadly that every impulse and every mental action will come under it. But then one must draw a distinction between aggressive and other feelings, and between different meanings of the word *force*.

If conceptual insight and violence together comprise the whole of the human being, there is no alternative in rhetoric between various faces of conceptuality on the one hand and open, concealed, or sublimated violence on the other. There is then probably no third place, for speaking and writing as *art*. Perhaps it is the task of a good rhetoric (and an aesthetic) to show that our emotional life cannot be split up into "rationality" and war. For a theory of discussion, this will mean that ways of speaking other than the systematic and polemic will have to be discussed: the varieties of speech typical for love, contemplation, desire, enchantment, and so on. All these ways of speaking, and their emotional sources, would need to be analyzed if one were attempting to develop a theory of truth-oriented conversation.

2.5 *The time structure of conversation*

A necessary condition for conversation is time. I must "take (the) time" for a conversation.

To speak with another is to alternate as speaker (who has the word and the authority) and as listener (who is receptive and obedient). As long as my word is law, the other follows my lead. But his time will come too. After I am finished, the other will have (the power of) the word.

The temporality characteristic for conversation is not a homogeneous and indifferent succession of one's own word followed by the other's, but is rather a series of phases, in which the *in*equality of speaker and listener(s) expresses and hears itself. Speaking time is scanned by the repeated exchanging of inequality, which *can* result in unanimity, but not in a supratemporal *logos* that makes all talking superfluous. The truth has often been represented as just such an authoritative *logos*: the concept of all concepts beyond all temporality and deliberation — a permanent now. In the light of eternity, this concept stands alone. It ends all discourse. Even its formulation in the form of a monologue is a form of degeneration, however, because it uses time — that is, it falls into the dispersion of the one-after-another and the outside-oneself. True Understanding stops all discussions and silently enjoys the One that is everything.

Imperialistic speakers boast of the timeless authority of eternal truth. They have no time to listen because they have nothing to learn. As soon as the other speaks, they either begin to refute, or to integrate, the speaker's words. In the latter case, they point out that the other does not sufficiently understand his own statements, which can only have a satisfactory meaning if they are transformed into parts of the true system. A transposition of the other's words into the conceptual and terminological patterns of the ruling speaker is then necessary.

Since time conditions the inequality between you and me,[15] it is a condition for the nonimperialistic speaking that we called "conversation." It is, however, still more. Temporality permeates our thought and makes it discursive, not only in the sense of a monologue proceeding step by step but also as a dialogue combining the plurality of times. The time structure that rules speaking turns our thoughts into phases of a history of words. This has consequences for the understanding of philosophical systems and their history.

3. Is philosophy a conversation?

Various aspects of truth-oriented conversation have been illuminated. The subject, as we have seen, is broader than the concept of "philosophical dialogue." The number of speakers was not thematized, and although philosophy was sometimes used as an example, the characteristics distinguishing philosophy from other kinds of truth-loving discourse were not discussed.

It is not necessary to explain the specific differences of philosophy here nor to compare them with other kinds of linguistic behavior. However, three aspects of philosophy are important within the context of this book:

1. A philosophy exists, for the most part, in the form of texts.
2. The language of philosophical treatises is governed by rules, which have their own history and are partly traditional, partly original.
3. A thematic philosophy is something other than a fleeting "word," leaving no trace of itself.

The second aspect is discussed below in sections 3.7 and 4. The first and the third are important for understanding the metaphorical character of the word *conversation*, as applied to an existent multitude of philosophers. They are discussed in sections 3.1 and 3.4.

3.1 Thematic philosophy and conversation

With the expression *thematic philosophy* we summarize an entire *oeuvre*. An *oeuvre* may come from a desire to take part in philosophical life, or from a need to reply to other philosophers. It is a whole composed of arguments, even if it consists of unfinished fragments or indications of a possible system. The philosophy produced in the course of a lifetime (or of a period) is a monument that we can inherit — a tomb in which the author's living voice is buried. It is not part of a fleeting dialogue but is rather a lasting composition, summarizing an entire history of formulations, It is condensed time. *We* scrutinize what someone has achieved in philosophy, take his products as a whole, and call them "Plato's philosophy," "the philosophy of (the early) Wittgenstein," "the philosophy of (the later) Kant." And *we* can consider such a philosophy as a contribution to our discussion. The analogy is not totally arbitrary, since philosophers themselves thought in response to questions of their own time and of other philosophers (of various periods). They experienced their own philosophies as contributions to the knowledge of others. Their formulations resemble the little speeches that comprise a whole discussion. That their life's work becomes one whole and is understood as a contribution to a discussion depends on our "listening" to it as a spoken "word," although it may consist of a series of texts that we read and study over a long, often interrupted, period of time. In the explicit discussion that takes place between philosophers, the word *discussion* is used in a less metaphorical sense. But even their polemics are usually meant to be more than just a word to another speaker. The public character of their writings shows that they are addressing themselves to a larger and unknown public, beyond those directly spoken to — often beyond their deaths, to posterity.

Since thematic philosophy is not a fleeting word but is tightly condensed time, it is not bound to its textuality. An oral presentation can also summarize an entire history of thought and inaugurate a long period of reflection. In a certain sense, *every* serious word is the result of a long history, but a spoken word vanishes: it exists only in a multitude of partial and transformed memories. Texts offer greater resistance to the changing and destructive forces of time. They remain present in their materiality, but demand new and forceful (re)thinking to live again. They also change through interpretation, although they regulate this with a steadier hand than do the remnants remembered from the spoken word. The spoken word, on the other hand, is better suited for forcing the listener to independency. The live presentation of a thinker can also be more stimulating, especially to beginners (and who is not a beginner?), than texts, since these suggest nothing unless someone makes them speak.

3.2 *Thematic philosophy and the history of philosophy*

If we can understand the actual multiplicity of thematic philosophies analogously to a living discussion, and if discussion is characterized by a specific time that disturbs the illusion of a timeless concept or eternal *logos* (cf. section 2.5), it is difficult, if not impossible to separate thematic philosophy from the history of philosophy. From the very beginning, then, every thematic philosophy is a part of the historical discussion. It is a fragment to be discussed, a contribution to further conversation.

In this context it does not matter whether one speaks of contemporary philosophy or of philosophy of the past. It makes no essential difference whether "word" and "reply" are separated from one another by a short or a long time. The time spent waiting for an answer is henceforth a moment of the thematic philosophy itself. The "ancients" are just as relevant to present philosophizing as are the strongest contemporaries, and more relevant than the less significant thinkers of the day. The situation, and presuppositions, of philosophy have changed, and we cannot get around this fact. But great intellectual differences and a lack of affinity can also occur between contemporaries.

In viewing all thematic philosophy as a moment in a discussion, our consideration shifts to a reflection on the history of philosophy (section 4). However, it is still possible to concentrate on the *parts* composing the historical Conversation, without explicating the historical relations of these parts.

3.3 *The abolition of the individual subject*

A current objection to the suggested analogy is raised in connection with its (inter)subjective and individualist character. If we see thematic philosophy as part of a discussion, do we not necessarily presuppose that it is totally the product of one individual, possibly even the self-expression of a most individual subject?

According to the above-mentioned objection, we have minimal interest in all the various things an individual experiences, thinks, and says. Philosophy is concerned with the meaning and the tenability of what is said. Its content survives after the author dies. What the living can do with it will become clear through interprettion. The speaker is not interesting; what he said may be.

Now the objection becomes particularly awesome. Who or what is the source and carrier of speech? Is the philosophical meaning of sentences and treatises the work of an individual user of language, or is the latter a mouthpiece, translator, or scribe for something else "speaking" or "writing" through him? Language itself, a certain culture, the spirit of a particular time, a people, a class, the structure of a certain society, the repressed eroticism of the unconscious are considered the origin of thematic philosophy, and not a unique philosopher's individual Ego. The individual subject participates semiconsciously, at best, in the process of language production; its language usage, too, is characterized by a powerless passivity.

The history of ideas is an old, spiritualistic version of this attack on the creative I. It presupposes that it is not the philosopher but rather the idea, that expresses itself in thematic philosophies and in their history. As the idea that comprehends itself, it is Spirit: the spirit of a people, or the world spirit, which gives itself a history by unfolding and then recollecting itself. Current versions of antisubjectivism base themselves on psychoanalysis, sociology, history, linguistics, semiotics, and so on. Proceeding from various behavioral sciences, they elevate insights into the process and structure of certain mechanisms to basic and all-encompassing social and historical principles. The modern celebration of freedom as autonomy has been replaced by the postmodern emphasis on anonymous structures, in which the individual subject sees himself caught.

A philosophy is thus not a speaker expressing himself but is rather an exponent of something else that conditions it. The life and work of a philosopher and the existential aspects of an *oeuvre* are no longer important. The thinker himself has nothing to say; he only plays a role. He finds himself on the stage, but we do not know who wrote his lines. There is no director.

3.4 *Conversation and text*

For those who maintain antisubjectivism, another concept is more relevant than the concept of conversation: every thematic philosophy consists, at least partially, of *texts*. The oral expressions added to them are either unimportant, or may be understood as a spoken text. In the last case, the word "text" is perhaps used metaphorically; in the other cases it literally presents the materiality, the "having-been-engraved" of actually existent philosophizing. Every philosophy is a collection of texts with some mutual relation, and the history of philosophy is a weaving together of texts, invoking and corresponding, or conflicting, with one another. Philosophy is a Text of texts, a Context and Intertext, a polyphony with the character of textuality.

From the textual perspective, the dialogical conception of philosophy appears to be an expression of narcissism. The thinker does not step away from his philosophy but wants to stay, to assist it. Have I produced something strong enough? The subject is afraid and wants to guarantee the victory of his ideas by raising his voice and producing powerful arguments. The fact that philosophizing consists in producing texts, however, means that the thinker may disappear. The text is a tombstone — and that is all right. To write is to make oneself superfluous; it prepares for one's disappearance. In a sense, every work is posthumous. Once a thinker has given us his work, information on his life adds as little meaning or value to it as information on an architect's feeling and vision adds to the sense and value of the building he has designed. The thinker himself can perhaps still provide service as an interpreter. But insofar as his explanation does not produce new texts, it is only a *mise en scene* of the work, which has left him behind.

In some respects the writing of a text corresponds to speaking. A thinker uses time to formulate what must be said about certain experiences and problems carefully. The possibility of going back to past utterances, however, is much greater here. In speaking, too, one can correct what does not seem altogether true in a later evaluation and can thus give new meaning to words spoken earlier. But one cannot take back what has been heard in a discussion; it continues to play the role of an earlier statement that has now been changed. The publication of a text does not reveal all the events and stages of its production. James Joyce spent more than 1200 hours on *Anna Livia Plurabelle*. But this past history does not play (or scarcely plays) any role in deciphering its textual fabric.

After a word has been spoken, it exists only as a possible memory. This presupposes that a listener has paid attention to it and internalized its form or meaning. Its continued existence requires an ever-renewed remembering and reproduction, actualizing a past present. The word can go on existing because someone understands it. (This person can also be the speaker himself, but then he has changed into one who has listened to himself.)

Texts have a permanence that makes them independent of the coincidental subject who remembers them. Remembering a text is more difficult than remembering a discussion (which is also easily distorted). The former, however, is less necessary because the written is an objective given, a part of the historical inheritance, a document that we can study again from beginning to end.

However, the difference between word and text is not as great as it seems. A text does not exist as a meaningful argument until a reader absorbs it and rethinks what the text "gives" him to ponder. By themselves the letters "give" nothing. In a sense the reader gives himself thoughts based on the text. He allows the marks on the page to regulate the formation of his thoughts. Another causes the dead text to live, the written to speak. (It can also be the writer who rereads "himself," but then he is another for himself-as-writer.) The awakening of a text is *lectura* and *interpretation*. Text and interpretation are inseparable moments of philosophy's "existence."

Both the spoken and the written word, then, only exist when appropriated by another — the reader or listener. He appropriates them within the limits of his own possibilities (which can be greater or lesser than those of the speaker or writer). Such an appropriation formulates the text or speech anew. It allows the interpreted text to "speak," insofar as it causes a thoughtful presence, here and now. The meaning of a text includes the existence of a present thinking of this text. Writer and reader are not exponents of an anonymous structure but are rather thinkers communicating with each other. The text regulating their communication, however, cannot be reduced to an invisible instrument for their reciprocal understanding. In re-reading my own text I am astonished: I have brought something into existence that is not altogether mine. The reader recognizes much of what he is concerned with and already suspected or knew; its newness exists not only in the other's thoughts but also in the textual suggestions and traces that a good reader perceives, without being obliged to know whether I, as writer, thought them myself. Through interpretation, a text continues to live in a transformation of its possibilities, and this transformation is a new text, which can itself, in turn, make history. Texts that are continuously commented on thus achieve immortality. Their meaning "lives," thanks to the responses of a thinking actuality — that is, thanks to others who here and now say or write what can still be thought from inscriptions of the past. Interpretation and reinterpretation are the posthumous effects of great thinkers. And here, too, everything depends on the existence of good readers.

In comparing speech and text, we have seen that the realization of their meaning demands, in addition to the author, at least one other who takes up his product and brings it to life in a personal way. Both text and speech are junction points of communication. In the simplest example of a conversation, the participants communicate in a very immediate way: the meaning exists as a sound that is simultaneously a speaking and a hearing. Even in this example, however, the hearer's appropriation of the message demands time. A text can bridge centuries and millennia, but it presupposes at least a minimal identifiability with the situation in which it was written. Between the extremes of an immediate presence and a retaking of prehistoric inscriptions, middle forms of temporality exist in speaking as well as in writing. In addition to the material fixation, a form of internalizing and remembering is also demanded in every communication.

If the remainder of this book presents thematic philosophizing and the history of philosophy as conversation, the point of this metaphor is the elucidation of a communicative structure, through which the *otherness*, as well as the *quality*, of philosophies can be both understood and practiced without becoming dissolved in a "dialectical" synthesis. The word *conversation* encompasses speaking, listening, appropriation, interpretation, and answering, and as a metaphor it is a resume of the parts comprising the history of philosophy. Since the greater part of philosophy exists in the form of texts, we might give our preference to a description putting the textual aspect in the foreground. Is there an expression that synthesizes the whole process of writing, publishing, reading, interpreting, digesting, and writing a new text? The word *textuality* is not only uncommon, abstract, and vague but it also gives the impression that philosophy could get along without individual thinkers and their intersubjectivity. The terms *textual communication* or *confrontation* might perhaps be acceptable, but they give rise to misunderstandings just as the other metaphor, *conversation*, does.

3.5 *Unmaskings*

The comparison of discussion and text distracted our attention from the objection cited in section 3.3. The attack on the individual subject by behavioral scientists with philosophical pretensions is probably the central problem of contemporary philosophy and its relation to the empirical sciences. An easy answer — for example, that the sciences are unable to answer philosophical questions — is not sufficient, even if it is correct. Philosophy must ask itself how it should react to the dismantlings and unmaskings proposed by psychoanalysis, linguistics, sociology, and history. What until recently seemed to be very original and spiritual (and even divine) is now exposed as a reversion to vulgar, and even suspicious, motives. What does this mean for philosophical selfexamination?

A thorough reflection on this problematic falls outside the scope of this work. I shall limit myself to a few remarks on three aspects of the struggle, insofar as this struggle is important for the nature of systematic philosophy. These three aspects are:

1. The unmasking of a (semiconscious or unconscious) lack of genuineness in philosophies that take themselves to be explanations of the truth (this section);

2. The statement that every philosophy is the expression of a hidden will to power (section 3.6);

3. The relation between the individual subject and the nonindividual, collective, or anonymous powers and structures that govern it (section 3.7 and chapter 4).

To designate a certain philosophy as not genuine does not contradict the idea that philosophy, rather than being the work of a thinking individual, is the product of anonymous superindividual or subindividual powers, mechanisms, processes, or structures. The lack of genuineness would, then, not consist of a philosopher's conscious lies, but rather of the "objective" fact that his words simultaneously express his thoughts and something that contradicts those very thoughts. The selfconscious thinking of such a philosopher exposes conscious or semiconscious narcissism, will to power, distorted social relations, linguistic reflexes, and so on.[16]

Marx, Nietzsche, and Freud have shown that many arguments on justice and love only appear to be inspired by a love for justice and love. They indicate an inner discrepancy between the content of an argument and the "real" intentions concealed in it, although the arguing subject is unaware of them. "Law and order" are defended and legitimized as law and good order *because* they guarantee the fundamental injustices of this order. Morality is preached out of revenge, sadism, or other immoral motives. Religion is a hedonism that denies itself.

On the level of theory, the indicated discrepancy is a contradiction between what is consciously said and what is unconsciously or semiconsciously intended. But a philosophy is not a matter of mere theory. It is moved by a *feeling*. The actual intention, the hidden motivation for the argumentation, comes forth from an impulse or "will," which can take on all sorts of forms: libido, greed, lust for domination, will to power, and so on. By revealing the suspected motives of a philosophy, one can make the value of its message suspect. But what kind of jurisdiction are we dealing with here?

It is clear that the value of evidence does not stand or fall on the purity of motive ruling a witness. Psychoanalytical and ideologically critical insinuations are not answers to the question whether philosophical statements are true. Even scoundrels sometimes speak the truth. And everything a critic says about other philosophers also applies to himself. What feeling, what sort of "will" or "desire," controls his judgement and theory?

Where does the *pathos* of unmasking, which delights so many unmaskers, come from? Does the pleasure of revelation have something to do with disappointment, revenge, cynicism, and resentment? Or does it spring from pure indignation at injustice and inauthenticity? Even self-revelation is no proof of honesty; it can be more morbid than the philosophies it criticizes as hypocritical.

If the motives of the critic may be just as questionable as those of the criticized philosophy, it seems necessary to ascertain the conditions necessary for a clean fight. It is not enough for a critic to become aware of his hidden motives. No one becomes better through knowledge alone. But what standard can the critic use to judge whether the motives guiding him, or another philosopher, are pure? For instance, if he condemns certain philosophies as egotistic, does he base his judgements on a norm prescribing love for others, or on one prescribing a superindividual well-being? If so, then that norm can be formulated as a theory of the good. But this must be investigated with the same Argus eyes of every other philosophy. The criticism of philosophy thus indicates the necessity not only of examining but also of purifying, the emotional foundations of a philosophy — a necessity that is possibly more important for the critic than for those he criticizes.

Have the great critics themselves not taught us how dangerous it is to want to be a judge? The moralism that so gladly judges is itself a disguise for the lust to dominate that triumphs even when it acquits. To be simultaneously judge, plaintiff, and claimant is just as delightful as being a philosopher who speaks in the name of the *Weltgericht*. Criticism and self-criticism are not necessarily "evil," but an absolutizing of the critical viewpoint suffers from an inability to take reality as it is, as does every absolutizing righteousness.

The norm of philosophy and philosophical criticism is love for the truth itself (cf. chapter 4). But if one considers "the truth" to be nonsensical or impossible, where will one seek a guideline? Is "genuineness" still possible if one gives up the idea of truth? Like honesty in the experiencing and rendering of facts as they actually are (a sort of fact truth), genuineness cannot be separated from the truth. How can honesty be ascertained and strived for? When it functions as a criterion, it comes from a specific morality and can be formulated as an ethics. But this implies the pretension that one is saying something true. If the relativism of truth seeks a solution to its contradictions in the rejection of genuineness and fraudulence — for example, through the thesis that those words no longer mean anything because there is no objective reality in man himself with which he has to agree — the whole pathos of unmasking becomes senseless. "Unmasking" is, then, an inadequate word. One can continue to expose the nontheoretical factors that play a role in philosophical positions; but there is absolutely no reason to find one position better than another.

Ideological criticism usually charges that the criticized philosophy *pretends* to defend truth, morality, justice, and so on, but *is* secretly untrue, immoral, and unjust. When the accusation is put in this way, the criticism indicates an *agreement* with the expressed intention of the philosophy in question. The fault of this philosophy would be that its pretension is false. Justice, the good, truth, and honesty are good according to the critic, too, but the criticized philosophy does not take its own ideals seriously. The criticism is, then, at least implicitly, an apology for the criteria that the accused philosophy professes but does not apply. This apology can be worked into a positive philosophy of truth, justice, and so on. If the criticism remains purely negative, its objects and implicit norms must be tracked down and judged by a metacriticism. If the criticism poses a *new* criterion or ideal, it does the same thing as the preceding philosophies; they must be compared according to the quality of its ideals and its theoretical arguments. The criticisms of philosophy are never immune to a critical distrust of their own pretensions and motives. *In all cases, they themselves involve a moral perspective, and thus, their own claims for truth.* If, after examination, a criticism appears to be true and pure, it is obviously possible to practice philosophy in a proper way. The struggle between "philosophy" and contemporary demystifications thereby become one more stage in the history of philosophy.

3.6 *Thematic philosophy and rhetoric*

According to some authors, philosophy is necessarily rhetorical. This epithet is usually taken in a restricted sense, as indicating the will to power that supposedly motivates every philosophy (cf. above, p. 87 ff.). Philosophizing is thus seen as an attempt to achieve non-logical effects — particularly the subjugation of others by verbal and logical means. Philosophical theories always involve apology, polemics, and *strategy.*

Philosophy exercises power in a typical way. Through the development of a theory (i.e., of a verbal and logical coherence), one shows the reader or listener that he can — and (if he is rational) must — see that this theory is correct. It is self-evident for one who is not stupid or foolish. Anyone who does not see this is irrational. In its usually suggested and sometimes explicitly formulated criticism, every philosophical theory is a moralistic and authoritarian ruse: if you do not agree with this (my) philosophy, you are not rational. This ruse is a perpetuation of violence. Theory is power and subjugation. Every philosophy is an ideology.

Some philosophers do not help the situation when they no longer condescend to support their claims with arguments but simply announce their statements with aplomb and contempt. Some of them defend their non-methods in the name of the idea that philosophy is a mere battlefield: the only thing that matters is achieving effects. Theories are only quasi-rational maskes for conflicting forces; arguments are war games. Asking the question of truth is a way of capitulating to a greater force. "When one wonders whether a philosophy is right or not, one is already subject to the power of censorship . . . ."[17]

If philosophizing is indeed a struggle for power, various possibilities are open to us. First, one contends that philosophy aims at nothing more than power. This standpoint can be practiced and justified in a trivial way, as Plato shows in his caricatures of Gorgias and other sophists. A more sophisticated version of the identity is possible, however. According to Spinoza, the highest force and power are *the* characteristics of the highest truth. The test of strength taking place in philosophical investigations results in the truth; this reveals itself and acquires power through its own force.

However, one can also recognize the rhetorical element in all philosophy without identifying power with truth. Even if a philosophy, according to a correct but limited viewpoint, is an ideology, at the same time it is whatever ideas and arguments an intelligent and truth-loving thinker reads into it. The question of these arguments' correctness or incorrectness is different from the question of their power. Stupid people and imposters often have a lot of influence. The truth of the greatest philosophers (such as Spinoza) often has little effect. According to Kierkegaard, one of the main characteristics of the truth is that is does not win; it suffers.

Still, such a separation of truth and power does raise difficulties However convincing their nonidentity may seem, to a thought in search for the ultimate, force appears to be a property of the truth. What do we mean by a "forceful theory"? Is it one that can stand firmly and defend its strength against many objections? What enables a philosophy to resist attacks and to impose itself on other minds? Is truth not necessarily experienced as something deserving obedience, respect, and submission, although it certainly does not enslave? Is truth a force that must impose itself and "rule" the person who desires to realize himself fully?

The problem of the relations between philosophy and rhetoric cannot be solved without a thorough reflection on the essence of truth and its relation to power and force. A part of this is the philosophical consideration of the relation between philosophy and politics. But a thorough reflection goes deeper and develops into a fundamental philosophy, or metaphysics. Plato's polemic against the political and "philosophical" (i.e., sophistical) fashions of his time remains exemplary.

3.7 The individual and the powers

This book's central theme is the intersubjectivity of philosophizing. One could call it a defense of philosophical conversation or dialogue, on the conditions that one (1) does not limit such a conversation to two speakers and (2) takes the word *conversation* metaphorically. All philosophies can be brought into discussion with one another; even philosophers who do not take notice of others can be read as participants in a history of speaking and writing that is not merely collective or anonymous but is rather a drama performed by individual thinkers. The following chapter will continue to defend this schema. The anthropological and ethical perspective defended by this book can hardly escape a discussion of the thesis that — as Foucalt quite sensationally put it — "man is dead." A thorough discussion of the opposition between human subjectivity and anonymous structures is not possible here, but we cannot omit a clarification of the problem and a certain justification of the standpoint taken in this book.

The structures of society and culture, the rules of language, mythology, and art, the historical constellation in which we find ourselves, and so on, condition the behavior and speech of individuals. As a social and historical power, philosophy too is governed by objective rules and reflexes. It conforms to a certain way of speaking that has been customary since 600 B.C. The thinking of individual philosophers and their exchanges are controlled by regulations that no one invented. Speaking and writing are at best variations on given language forms. Some have tried to draw a distinction between *particular* forms of thought (determined by a specific context) and *universal* forms which structure all human thought a priori. Such a universality would salvage the meaning and capacity for truth of the individual thinker. What is necessary, then, is the formulation of a logic that differentiates the universally valid elements from the historically, socially, and biographically determined ones, which are also part of a philosophy. There is a strong suspicion in our century, however, that no universal logic of thought forms is possible, not only because the formulation of any logic is itself subject to all sorts of particularity but also, more principally, because there is no such thing as a suprahistorical structure of all true thought. Nothing escapes history, and history knows no constants. During a certain priod, the network of basic forms remains the same, but at a certain point, the system of this period is broken off and makes room for a radically different ground structure. If the rupture separating the two can be explained as a necessary or normal event, the discontinuity is not complete; if it is contingent, a philosophy of the transitions, and thus of history, is impossible.

According to the conception quoted here, a logic such as Hegel's, Kant's, or Leibniz's is the result of a certain epoch of thinking. In spite of great differences, often ignored, the logics of Hegel, Kant, and Leibniz are of the same family as those of Plato and Aristotle. But the basic structures of Greco-Western thought are not universal either. The patterns composed by these structures dominated 2500 years of history. They can be described as "onto-theo-logical thinking" (Heidegger) or as "egology" (Levinas). But such a diagnosis of its particularity is also a death notice.

What has been described here on the basis of the concepts *structure* and *history* can also be formulated on the basis of language, the unconscious, or social relations. One can always show that an individual's life, language usage, and thought are the exponents of anonymous "powers," *not* of "*the* language," "*the* society," "*the* culture," "*the* history" — although this is the common way of talking — for these exist only in and as the speaking, the experience, the cultural behavior, and the personal history of individual people. One can, however, defend the notion that the conscious and unconscious actions of individuals are codetermined by certain impersonal *elements* of society, culture, and so on.

What is the content and the nature of this domination "undergone" by the individual? Which powers are too strong, even for a philosopher, and how can he understand their "causality"? The question of the content of what is thought "under influence" belongs, to a great extent, to the behavioral sciences. Philosophy has much to learn from them, as a central part of the philosophy of science. The question of the "causality" of nonindividual factors in individual behavior is for science and philosophy together to consider. A philosophy of the relations between individuality and intersubjectivity cannot be satisfied by the juxtaposition of a subjectivistic and a structuralistic viewpoint; such a philosophy should at least make it plausible that in spite of *and thanks to*, the anonymous powers regulating, structuring, and ruling him, an individual can realize *himself*.

The introspective consciousness of our freedom is vulnerable because so much evidence has turned out to be illusory. Still, immediate evidence remains an essential criterion. Otherwise, how could we prove that the supposed evidence is illusory? How else except on the basis of other, more solid evidence? But is there authentic and irrefutable evidence of individual autonomy? Or are we victims of the Western and, in particular, the modern way of feeling?

A more external approach seeks for the trace of individuality in the peculiar *style* with which every person distinguishes himself. But is the attention given to originality (e.g., in the form of hero worship) not a relic of romanticism? How can the uniqueness of each individual be distinguished from a *universal* peculiarity and individuality characteristic of all human beings? Can we not imagine that the modern privatization of culture is again making room for a society in which all culture is common and in which heroism and originality no longer mean anything?

Even in the most collectivistic culture, I cannot escape the task of doing what must be done and saying what is correct *myself*. Even if everything were self-evident and everyone were expected only to conform to rules, I would still be irreplaceable and unique insofar as I accepted this activity (or this undergoing) *myself*. The *ought*, or in a broad sense of the term the moral viewpoint given with the difference between an individual and the instance that rules him, implies a certain form of *being-oneself*. It forbids a total reduction, or neglect of, one's individuality.

The "morality" spoken of here consists of the demands a society makes on its members. An individual is, however, more than just submissiveness. *If* there is *thinking* in a collectivistic society, some individuals at least must wonder about the meaning and the justification of its morality. These individuals question this society and in principle go beyond it — not to an individualism, but to the demand for a *justified* morality and society, which may be different from the established ones.

Criticism and transformation are not in themselves a refutation of all the objections to the individual's originality. It usually appears, at least in retrospect, that criticism and renewal are in no way creations *ex nihilo*: they exploit possibilities that are already present in the existing constellation. To be "creative" is to bring the waiting seeds to fruition. If you change the level and quality of a cutural system you are radically innovative, but the suggestions you take up are already there. In this respect your individual achievements are the products of the world in which you live.

There are enough arguments from the behavioral sciences to defend the thesis that a human individual is nothing more than an exponent or mouthpiece of something else. By reducing all originality to a junction point where a combination of given forces sorts out their effects, that thesis is absolutized. However, one can always reverse the roles and, with the support of immediate experience, maintain that the defense of the deterministic viewpoint (be it structuralist, archeological, collectivistic, or idea-historical) is the result of a choice. The reduction of individual subjectivity into something else is itself an individual view and choice. Nothing can destroy this interpretation of the structuralist behavior. For, which experience, which science, is stronger than the self-experience of an irreducible self? If this experience is an illusion, why are the experiences on which the reductionists base their interpretaions not illusory, but solid? Again, the absolutizing of a perspective destroys its (relative) truth.

If the viewpoints of originality and of anonymous structures can both be defended, it is a task for thought to understand them as perspectives — that is, as moments of one insight — or, if this is too difficult, at least to put forward their interrelation. The sciences overwhelm us with statistics and arguments to show the power of everything that we undergo. Until now, however, little attention has been paid to an analysis of science as the work of individual researchers or to the experiences, perspectives, and choices by which they became scientists. Husserlian phenomenology paid a great deal of attention to prescientific intentions and structures, but not much to the essential function of individuality within the scientific process.

The truth of the individual is not only found in the immediate self-experience of a self-conscious ego — concerning which the unmaskings and reductions discussed above have given us a bad conscience — but it also presents itself, and more objectively, in the experience of the other, to whom I am obligated.[18] Kant has already indicated the "experience" of respect as a way in which freedom makes itself known. The element of alterity characterizing ethical experience frees our apology for selfhood from its narcissism. But it is not only another person who overcomes me; my own humanness overcomes me as an other to whom my life, and thus my thought, is oriented. If ethics is of any value — how could we otherwise escape from a world in which the "right" of the strongest is correct and in which philosophy and every use of language is only cunning? — it is impossible to reduce our speech to the pure product of an anonymous force. Speaking is also ruled by another alterity that is not reducible to narcissism, to sado-masochism, to class interests, to cultural fixations, and so on. If ethics is anything at all, then human individuals are irreplaceable.

The moral "passivity" effected in me by *this* other (In the form of another human being and also as an aspect of the humanness imposed on me as a task to be carried out)[19] liberates me from absolute determinism and gives me my moral, and therefore my anthropological, independence. Although "It thinks" ("It speaks," "It writes") contains a certain truth, just as "I think" (and speak and write), I am not really free for independent thought (and speech and writing) until I am "addressed" by the other (in the other or in myself).

4 The history of philosophy as conversation

4.1 *Text and author*

Since the philosophers and philosophies treated in a history of philosophy are for the most part hidden in a series of texts, they must be recalled by good readers before they can figure in a new text describing their history.

Since in a conversation a word exists at one and the same moment both as spoken and as heard, speaker and listener are unified if they understand this word in the same way. A text separates author and reader by a period of time that can have lasted for many years and have bridged many generations. What was written can have been left behind and covered with dust. As the result of conversation (with others and with oneself), a text already contains many corrections that have come out of preceding dialogues. As a report on the conversations that have prepared it, a text can have the character of a summary. As the culmination of a verbal history, it has the tendency to look back and to reflect on its past. The author is already somewhere else: if he does not persevere in the repetitions and applications of his writings, he has grown beyond them and is preoccupied with finding new and different thoughts.

The inevitable distance between the writer and his text is responsible for the particular kind of distance that separates him from his readers. The difficulties involved in understanding a text are evidence of the inner distance that thinking must bridge before reader and author can meet. A text does not speak for itself. It must be brought to speak, and this is always a *bringing back* of the living thinking crystallized within it. "What did the author intend here?" "To what is he alluding?" "To which elements of his situation is he referring?" "How can he say such a thing?" A text continues to give evidence of thinking, and thus of the thinker from whom it derives its existence. We sometimes need to know very little about the life and peculiarities of an author, but even with an anonymous author, we cannot make a total abstraction of the intention that inspired his text. *Someone* directs himself to us, his unknown readers. The assertion that the author's intention may be forgotten altogether because the text presents the *noema* in itself is incomprehensible. A *noema* is nothing unless it is actually, virtually, or potentially intended by someone. If this "someone" is a reader bringing the text to life through his own intention, he produces a new *noema* based on the text: his way of understanding the written words. To this extent the text is a potential, or virtual, *noema* of a new living intention.

The question of how the intentions (and corresponding *noemata*) of author and reader are related must be asked and (at least approximately) answered. If they have *nothing* to do with each other, we cannot speak of interpretation. In this case, for example, Spinoza's *Ethica* is no longer Spinoza's thought, but rather a puzzle to be solved without even asking what it means or intends to say. This comparison is not altogether correct, because even a puzzle is assembled by someone who intends something, namely, to conceal the right answer. If the author no longer plays any role, one must compare "his" text to a natural phenomenon such as a composite crystal or a bird song or the rustling wind, about which others can form their thoughts. The absolutizing of textuality results in a general proclamation of death: not a single author can have anything to say; his words are part of a silent nature that surrounds us. Orphaned and alone, we possess the monopoly of language. Everyone may think what he pleases of the riddles given him in stone and script; our desire for communication is just as pious and illusory as the immortality aspired to by any writer. Whoever writes down his thoughts merely adds new scratchings to the graffiti of an old world, without any hope for survival.

The distance imposed by the text between writer and reader is not absolutely different from the one separating participants in a discussion. The fact that a listener quickly understands a speaker can obscure the fact that the words spoken and the words heard are not simply identical but rather differ in how they are being thought. A spoken word is a thought that the speaker thinks, or tries to think, and puts into words more or less precisely. To digest it, the listener must allow it to sink in. If the word is unusual or difficult, its integration takes time and work: a thinking effort to reproduce what was offered as a thought to be thought about. Of course, with regard to spoken words too, the listener can be less interested in the speaker's thoughts than in the new speeches that can be made out of the semantic and syntactical material he is hearing. Whoever conceives of the history of philosophical utterances in this way sees them as a collection of building blocks, or as grammatical and lexical elements to be used for the construction of new texts. History, then, would be no more than a larder of material for other, unique philosophies.

4.2 *Interpretation*

A text does not say anything unless a reader brings it to "life" or causes it to "speak." A text "speaks" or"lives" if it stimulates someone to think about what he reads. "Written thoughts" must now exist in the thinking of their readers and no longer in the thinking of the writer as writer, for the latter has passed away with his inscriptions. In (re)reading my own texts, I rediscover what I thought at an earlier stage of my existence. Although I may still agree with my former thoughts, there is a difference not only in time, but also in the thoughts that separate my writing from my reading. As a reader I, too, am forced to reconstruct what I have thought. Sometimes I still remember what I thought while I was writing, but this is not an absolute criterion for the interpretation of my texts, because it is not certain that my formulations were adequate. The text "speaks" for itself (if someone brings it to speak). As a writer I must change myself into a reader and interpreter if I want to explain my own creations. Since I carry my past with me, my ideas preserve a certain relationship with the ideas I tried to record in writing. This qualifies me as an exegete who is closer to my texts than many others. Notwithstanding my being bound to a particular past, I may have left my earlier thoughts behind me, so that my own writings have become foreign to me. Others might now understand them better.

Since a text requires a "someone" in order to be meaningful, a philosophical treatise must be read and understood if we are to say that it "contains" ideas. The support a text needs in order to "say" something[20] can seldom be given by its producer. In any case the author, too, stands at a greater or lesser distance from his text. The explanation of what is "written" is a new formulation of suggestions, in the form of mute signs waiting to be actually thought (or to be real thoughts). By understanding them, a reader reproduces the results of a preceding completed production. He lends a thoughtful presence to words that have "survived" their first life. In explaining them, he translates "with other words" (his own) what the author has left behind. Since the bond with the author can never be totally severed, every explanation is also an *apologia* or *oratio pro alio*. However, as a *re*production and actualization, it is a new text, for which the apologist is partially responsible.

The presentation of a text is a re-presentation: a wording that is different from the originally presented text. The distances between writer, text, and reader are expressed in this difference of language. How much may, or must, an interpretation vary from the text it is explaining? Copying or reciting may contribute to understanding, if it stresses articulations and accents in the text. A paraphrase that remains close to the author's terminology presupposes a certain familiarity with it and raises our suspicion that one would do just as well, or better, to read the original. By the conversion of a given text into another terminology, one runs the risks of not explaining "what the author wrote," and of writing a very different text. An explanation based on other theoretical presuppositions could very well bar, rather than open, the entry into a text.

There is no single, all-purpose norm for interpretation. However, the interpreter must know what he is doing.

His interpretation is excellent if it allows someone to make a better connection with the explained text than he had before. Interpretation, as a reading aid, aims at making itself superfluous. It gives the prerequisite historical and cultural information concerning the text; it shows the questions asked, the lines of the argument, the division of the text, the interconnections of the concepts used, and so on. The positivistic element of the history of philosophy systematizes this way of interpretation. It remains as close to the texts as possible, but at the same time it develops techniques for deciphering and — if it reflects on itself — a theory of deciphering. (This, then, is a part of thematic philosophy, namely, philosophical reflection on reading and interpretation and on the writing of history as a reconstruction of the period in which the texts were written.)

Instead of looking for explanations to ease our understanding of certain texts, we can also read them for no other reason than to find inspiration for new ideas of our own. From this perspective, earlier philosophies are merely stimulants. As a thematic philosopher, I make whatever I want out of them. The History of philosophy, then, functions only as a portal to genuine Philosophy. This way of reading is unfruitful if it does not carry me away from myself. If a text only confirms or denies what I already know, it does not further my insight. If it is not particularly well written, its reading is a waste of time. An all-knowing attitude prevents me from learning anything new and does not do justice to the original authors. It is possible, however, to expose myself to the otherness of a written thought with no other goal in mind than the production of my own philosophy. Other philosophers are there for me. My interpretation is part of my own train of thought. My interests are my standards for the selection and the way of reading through which old texts may acquire the actuality of living thought.

All sorts of gradations are possible between the two extremes of reading aid on the one hand and hermeneutical (re)creation on the other. We can speak of "interpretation" as long as two elements are present in some form and to some degree:

1. A reference to the text (already expressed by the fact that the words [the text] of the interpretation cannot exist in total separation from the interpreted text) is made; and

2. One's own thoughts are responsible for a noticeable distance between the letters of the text and the spirit of the interpretation given.

4.3 *An ethics of interpretation*

Aside from the art of reading and the hermeneutical techniques demanded by this art, the interpretation of a text presupposes a moral attitude. A sense of responsibility for the life and death of texts not only obliges me to integrate them into my own thought but also to perform a kind of service for their authors and other readers. I must do justice to the writer; his legacy must be handed over and, if necessary, explained to posterity, at least if the text is not stupid or vain or cheap or *itself* unjust and lacking in respect. Even if the text is bad, I must respect the dead author by not identifying him with his text.

Back in a time when there was not so much printed paper daily streaming into one's house, a written work could count on more respect than it now can. Our disappointment with many publications contributes to a distrust that is difficult to overcome when we attempt to convince others that they "must read" something. Some texts, however, have become sacrosanct as a result of thousands of readings, explanations, and evaluations; they attract attention, and one must be well advanced to maintain that they are unimportant or empty.

To say that a text is "all right" and "should be read" means the same. Whether a given text can be described as "all right" can only be known after it has been read. But in order to read it, one must at least surmise that it is worthwhile. A certain credit, a sort of hypothetical respect, is thus demanded *before* one decides to evaluate a text. By refusing to give it any credit, we would condemn a philosophy before it had had the chance to give its own evidence. Such a bias can come from partiality: the author belongs to another group; therefore he probably writes nonsense. But, was this group ever seriously listened to?

Taking your opponent seriously is the basis for a fair rendition of his writings. The "positivism" that was referred to earlier as an essential element of every history of philosophy is grounded in this. It cannot be based on the egological subject-object schema. Although this schema admits the necessity of leaving one's home and sojourning in a foreign territory (my own enrichment demands a confrontation with other philosophers), an egological confrontation prepares a final monologue. In it other philosophies are merely preliminary stages or subordinated elements. The other loses his uniqueness to the Ego's assimilation. A true *oratio pro alio* leaves open the possibility that I am not able to appropriate the other philosophy, although it still has its own value and right to exist. The attitude that this hypothesis claims seems to be a necessary condition in order for a fair history of philosophy to do justice to everyone. "Everyone" here means: everyone who has something to say that is worth reflecting on. But who determines whether a statement is worth reflecting on? As a historian I cannot avoid giving an evaluation, even if I only refer to what 'everybody," or other historians of philosophy, think about the value of certain philosophies. I myself still attach a value to the judgment of those others. The evaluation expressed by my selection does not, however, necessarily imply a monological intention, and I can always present my history of philosophy as one of many possible perspectives, which all equally contribute to "*the* history."

Besides being "positivistic," impartial, "neutral," and "objective," an interpreter must be an advocate or apologist for the texts upon which he concentrates. The ethics of reading does not stop at a careful reconstruction of the meaning "contained" in a text. Not only as a human being but also as an author, the author is more than his writings.

The identification of an author with his text kills him. This statement is not an apology for the subterfuge of those who claim to think or know more than they can write, but rather an admission of the fact that a writer never totally succeeds in writing what he intends to write. Every text is in some way a failure: the author was not able to say (and thus also not able to think) what he was seeking for. Texts are pointers, stones that mark the way, but thinking continues to aim at an unwritten and indescribable truth.

The best apology for a philosopher is an interpretation that presents his case as strongly as possible, even more strongly than do the letters of his own text. Such an interpretation supplements his work with arguments that are only indicated by the author and clarifies his intentions through information taken from his letters and conversations. Through such careful work, the historian sustains a philosopher's life and honor. He thus "saves" him from oblivion. As managers of an inheritance, historians of philosophy can determine how long an author lives, in contrast to the epigones, who keep repeating what has passed.

4.4 *Anonymous thought*

Must the history of philosophy direct itself in the future less towards philosophy and more towards currents, collective perspectives, and speaking styles, prejudices, schemas, and methods? They, too, "speak" in texts — but are they philosophical?

However original philosophies may be, they always involve perspectives and notions reflective of their times. Insofar as these have become integral parts of their works, the commonplaces shared by great thinkers with the people of their time belong to the content of the history of philosophy. Insofar as they represent the unreflected convictions of a speech-making community, however, they are not much more than everybody's opinions. In order to become acquainted with the theoretical quality of a particular time, it is important to track down the pattern of its prejudices. But a history presenting them as "the prevailing philosophy" would mistakenly identify philosophical thinking with the common sense of a particular group of people. It would neglect the *thought* character of philosophy and describe no more than the *milieu* in which and from which thinking lives. Many general viewpoints are documented by the media and by a great deal of essayist literature. If philosophical texts have merely reproduced commonly held views, they are only illustrations of beliefs that were held by many people during a certain period of time. By reducing all philosophies to such beliefs, one shows a total neglect of the philosophical features of philosophy. After all, commonly held opinions are characterized by the fact that they are not reflected on, let alone thought through; they are semiconsciously, almost automatically, taken over and propagated. "Anonymous thinking" is a contradiction of terms. Indeed, thinking starts when someone shrinks from the gratuitousness of everybody's convictions and wonders: what will I do with this in my own reflection and out of my responsibility for what is said? What can and must I make of it?

The explanation of a philosophy is greatly helped by an account of the milieu from which it originated and the materials available to it, but its thought can only begin to manifest itself at the point where that account ends. An archeology of the tracks, passageways, and structures through which historical philosophizing has been channeled prepares for a consideration of the philosopher's originality in integrating them. The transition from collective evidence to the actual thinking of one or more individuals is the ever-repeated birth of Philosophy. Although the history of philosophy is not a hero worship, it is a commemoration of unique achievements.

4.5 History of philosophy as a triumph

Many accounts of philosophical history present it as an uphill progression towards the true (or most nearly true) philosophy, against which all other philosophies must be understood as preparations, variants, or shadows. Artistotle, Kant, Hegel, Comte, Marx, and Russell have all used this schema in their own way. It is found in two forms, depending on whether the emphasis is placed upon authors or upon currents of thought.

If history consists of a series of philosophers, the kind of history mentioned above implies that there is a thinker who knows the truth better than all of his predecessors and colleagues. He must be capable of judging to what extent the others are right or wrong, and why. The philosopher in whom the history of thought culminates is the master assigning to all other philosophers their places and partial truths. He need not be the most recent philosopher, for the history after him may be a decadent one, deserving oblivion. The historian, however, must either be this true philosopher or an adept who swears by him. His norm is the one true thinker who throws light on the whole of earlier and contemporary philosophical activity. In neo-Thomistic circles, this sort of history is found rather often. It is peculiar to every epigonism but is equally characteristic of self-aware and competent philosophers for whom truth exists outside their own insights or opinions.

Another version of the evolutionary history we are criticizing here sees the philosophical process as an expression of a collective consciousness, or a superhuman spirit. It is a modern version of ancient and medieval notions concerning a higher Intellect, which in some way illuminates individual thinkers. Hegel and Marx are classic examples of this perspective, widely popularized by neo-Hegelian and neo-Marxist epigones.

In both versions, other philosophies are discussed only insofar as the one true (or truest) philosophy can either incorporate them as a subordinate section or unmask them as errors. The account is thus at the same time an evaluation; the historian has climbed onto the judge's bench. Like the rendition and evaluation of a philosophy, the evaluation of the historical constellation of philosophies can be given on many levels. A historian can take the standpoint that his world view, the perspective of the elite to which he belongs, or the conviction of the proleteriat sets the standard for the presentation of various philosophies. These, then, are reduced to the most superficial level of *opinion* and are consequently evaluated in terms of the simple maxim: "I (or we) agree (or do not agree)." The history of philosophy is subsequently transformed into a crusade for the only true faith.

A historian is more serious when he confronts a particular philosophy with certain *experiences* that do not correspond with its statements. The debate on the genuineness and truth of certain experiences that from the basis of a particular philosophical thought is *philosophically* interesting.

Paying attention to the *argumentation and method* of the various philosophies and to the *presuppositions* on which they are based brings one to the heart of historical philosophizing. Whoever thinks he has found the definitive method and correct logic from which he can judge the correctness of historical systems is either very naive or an exceptional genius who has finally solved the fundamental problems of philosophy. He is either as unaware as an animal, or he is more than a man: a god.

But even the logical and methodological starting points, and *a fortiori* the experiences in which philosophy puts its trust, depend on hidden sources, whose solidity must be tested by a contemporary account of such a philosophy. A radicalization of transcendental reflection, combined with insights from sociology, psychology, linguistics, and ethnology, looks beyond the explicit thoughts to the hidden, but effective, motives that have determined the nature and method of existing philosophies. If you engage in this metareflection, it is almost impossible, psychologically, to keep yourself out of the discussion in order to concentrate on the others in view of the one true or best philosophy. Whoever thinks deeply is more likely to fall into scepticism than to write a history of the true philosophy and its half-true and untrue counterparts.

The writer of such a history must not only be convinced that he is correct on all the levels mentioned above — the levels of *doxa*, of the *empirical*, of *logic*, and of the *hidden foundations* — he must also be sure that he sees the relations among these levels correctly. Once again, he must have solved the fundamental problems of philosophy. On this condition — that is, after ending the philosophical debate on "the principles" by finding the one true philosophy — a philosophical history is a mere summary of the truth itself, in which the only good thematic philosophy reveals itself in a chronological fashion.

The merit of dogmatic histories is that they show how their authors' thematic philosophies have incorporated ideas of their own time and of their past. The punishment for their naiveté is an overestimation of their own standards and an inability to learn anything new from the study of other ideas. The ease with which the self-assured knower selects, divides, gives names, evaluates, and categorizes is the reward for his failure to ask the questions that lie at the roots of the ever-old and ever-new Beginning.

4.6 *The history of philosophy as discussion*

Every historically aware thinker asks himself how his philosophy relates to the philosophies of the past. This backward look to his predecessors can be worked out into a history of philosophy sketching the rise of true philosophizing. But if the history of philosophy may not assume in advance that one particular philosophy is the true one, the various incompatible philosophies must be presented as independent, serious possibilities. An absolute neutrality is not possible, since the selection and degree of attention already given involve a judgment of the philosophies treated. But one can and must shed light on both the plausibility and the contestability of the thoughts presented. Instead of a self-chosen dogma that gives the history of philosophy an unambiguous direction, the possibility of contesting becomes a guideline for the historian of philosophizing. His description reveals history as a divergence of perspectives, foundations, ways of arguing, experiences, and conceptions. Very different descriptions are possible, but disagreements notwithstanding, they belong together within the community of thinkers who are seeking the same thing. If philosophies are worth mentioning, they all realize their search for truth in their own way and with their own degree of success.

If such a portrayal does not degenerate into a superficial tale of everything that has been said and written but is itself actuated by philosophical interest, it can very well function as an introduction and orientation to thematic philosophy. It does not present one system before which all others must bow, but rather divergence itself, as a constellation of related, and yet different, problematics and solutions. On the basis of such a description, the reader travels many paths. How much he brings home and incorporates from such a journey depends on the traveler, as well as on his guide.

As was stated earlier, every thematic philosophy is also historical insofar as all thinking needs time to come into being via attempts, corrections, renewed beginnings, and returns to starting points in order to do everything over again, and better. Because philosophizing is a radical way of thought, the discoveries made in this field force us to adjust our previous thoughts and earlier statements: to provide them with more nuances, to correct them, even to deny or reverse them. The progress of thematic thought, exploratory and reflective, is itself quite a story: its genesis is an essential component of all philosophy.

When this insight into the unbreakable bond between thinking and its genesis is applied to the whole of Western philosophy, it becomes clear that philosophy can be understood as one great attempt at thinking, by a multitude of subjects. The subjects, of course, do not always know one another — only a few philosophers have dealt with other philosopher's works — but the historian who examines their products can relate them as contributions to one continuous discussion. Insofar as they are all looking for approximately the same thing, they show a relationship to one another; because they seldom agree, their interrelation is also a disputation. If their belonging together has not been expressed in discussions with one another, it may be brought about by an external perspective asking questions, on which all of them are equally at work.

The idea of discussion, as it is analyzed in the preceding sections, can be applied to the historical constellation of philosophical constellations. Even if most philosophers have not entered into discussion with one another, *we* are able to bring their philosophies into a conversation, now. To do so, however, we must arrange their meeting and defend them from their own perspectives. At the same time we must be aware that our reconstruction of a past or distant philosophy occupies a new place in the ongoing conversation constituting the history of philosophy. The mere fact, for example, that an interpretation of Plato's works takes into account the present anti-Platonic climate already makes it different from Plato's thought. As I have already said, the way in which the historian presents the history of philosophy as a discussion is itself a philosophy. A self-conscious historian will therefore not present his view as the final word; he will not speak as a final judge, a philosopher, or a god but as someone who proposes one new (and not the last) contribution to the multisubjected discussion.

The "method" being defended here has little or nothing in common with the view that the past is a mere series of exercises leading to definitive solutions. Unfortunately, one hears many statements like the following, even from the mouths of famous people praised for their logical expertise: "We, in our time, have discovered that . . ." or "Twentieth-century philosophy has established that . . . — for example, that metaphysics is nonsense, that it is not worthwhile to philosophize about the infinite, that "essentialism" if something bad, and so on. If the authors of such expressions do not deign to give an intrinsic proof for the statement that they actually want to assert or deny via their "we" and "our time," they are assuming the authority of a particular "time" or group of people referred to as "we." The difficulties facing us when we do not simply want to make a claim but argue it are (1) that we must say what "our time" and "we" mean and (2) that we must explain why these bodies (if they are anything at all) have so much authority. Slogans such as "being modern" and "being progressive," "emancipation," "realism," and so on are not of any help here and will chase a serious listener away, unless the foundations and the real or assumed authority of these slogans are revealed. If it is permissible in philosophy to defend ourselves by the simple fact that "we" "think" it "nowadays," we no longer need to study history. We cannot learn anything from it, because it only represents a pre-history without any truth of its own. Of course, one can be curious as to how far we have come, and it is probably useful to know what mistakes were made earlier so that we can avoid repeating them, but learning, receptivity, gratitude, and rethinking have made room for the self-assuredness of a scientific actuality raising "our time" above all of its preparatory stages in the past.

If the "we" in this connection does not mean an elite but every Tom, Dick, and Harry, along with their commonly held opinions, we may again be reminded that such a "forum" is found on the level of commonplaces and superficial prejudices. But since when has the opinion of the majority, the force of the people (among whom many average "philosophers" can perhaps be counted) been a criterion for good philosophy? If the voice of the people is decisive, then philosophy is a part of sociology. Why should anyone still bother with philosophy if one is to think what everyman "thinks"? It might, of course, be interesting to analyze what is in, beneath, and behind it. Perhaps such an analysis would reveal inner contradictions and stupid assumptions, but if Everyman is king, philosophy changes into politics.

4.7 Teamwork in philosophy?

The subject matter of philosophy is the multitude of conversations that have taken place, or can be arranged by a historian, among all the historical thinkers who have made their thoughts known to others in oral or in written form. It is essential for a philosophical discussion that every participant assume responsibility for himself and for the success of the conversation. Is it possible to conceive of this conversation by the analogy of a laboratory where various individuals perform one job together, or of a joint deliberation aiming at a unanimous decision?

What can the word *we* mean when it is used in connection with the production and propagation of a philosophy?

"We think that . . . " can be said by the loyal members of a Party or a Church. In totalitarian systems, this is the only permissible way of speaking and writing. The power of the mass media can bring so-called philosophers to conform with opinions that most listeners would find self-evident. Even within the world of science and philosophy, there are temptations lying in wait: by being loyal to an authentic stream of thought, one risks missing out on honors and financial rewards. The lively fish that swims upstream is often devoured in public. Obedient "philosophers" do nothing except reformulate, clarify, and unfold what "they," the media, the current trends, the sciences, the authorities want to hear. They lack the courage for a critical examination of the unpondered, possibly unacceptable, presuppositions by which "the many" allow themselves to be ruled. For them, truth is a question of power and conquest: "philosophers" are only useful for selling imperatives and instructions in the form of dogmas.

Unanimity in "thinking" also occurs in Schools, where epigones of a great master unfold his ideas and exploit their possibilities. Notwithstanding the relative utility of their work, it also contains a great danger: a School can easily be taken over by a Church or a Party because epigones do not think independently. If you impose your individuality by means of critical and thorough thinking, you are beloved by neither the masses nor their guides. The very fact that you consider individuality and selfhood to be irreducible makes you a dissident.

Is a "forum of experts" possible in philosophy, as it is in other sciences? Every forum is based on a choice, and this rests on appreciations that result from a specific philosophy. Do we need another forum to establish the quality of these basic assumptions? Who is responsible for the selecting of the members who will comprise the highest court and for the laws by which they will evaluate the work of other philosophers? Is there a higher court than that of authentic philosophy itself?

A forum functioning as an authority for a certain conception or method is a secularized form of the old theological dogma. Just as apologetics formerly justified the authority of the Church, rational justification is now demanded for surrendering to the court of so-called experts. A philosopher is particularly interested in such a justification, not only because insight interests him more than authority but also because the basic questions must be answered *before* one determines who, in fact, is an expert. The definition of expertise in philosophy presupposes a good understanding and evaluation of philosophical techniques and results. Before I can appeal to a forum I must ask the question, what is good philosophy? But if I know the answer, the authority earlier attributed to a forum has been transformed: either its dogmatic authority has been deduced from a nonauthoritarian insight, which needs no forum, or that authority has been unmasked as an illegitimate pretension. In any case, the group of philosophers first to be proclaimed as judges now functions as one of the many seminars in philosophy. If I appeal to a forum before I have become a philosopher, I cannot know if I am appealing to the right group. Once I have come to know what philosophy is, I, too, take part in the family discussion — unless I know everything so well that I either possess the total truth (in which case I can appoint myself and my epigones to the tribunal of truth) or I have discovered with certainty (by deduction or revelation) who the true judges are.

A fourth kind of unanimity is also conceivable: the unanimity of an ideal society, united by a discussions held under the ideal conditions that lead to complete agreement. Chapter 4 will say more about this; for the moment it may suffice to state that such an ideal presents the classical idea of universal truth in a more concrete, albeit utopian, way while neglecting the problem of individuality. Its defenders seem to hope for a victory over the differences that make all speaking and writing individual, and thus debatable.

Every history of philosophy is characterized by a certain attitude towards the problematic of unity and plurality. An epigonal history introduces its hero as culmination and standard against the background of progress and decline. Totalitarian histories are masked dogmatisms that reduce every heresy to an error, or a subordinate moment of history. The irreducibility of pluralism, defended by a dialogical conception of history, destroys all-encompassing syntheses and final judgments. Because thinking means thinking *for oneself*, it remains an individual and lonely work. Accordingly, the collaboration of various authors on one work is impossible. Teamwork is not a philosophical method. This fact, however, does not exclude the existence of a common resource and of all kinds of relationships. But they are concerned with the preparations *preceding* actual thought. They result from a converging of thought processes and constitute material to be assimilated and transformed by individual thinkers, after study and debate.

The milieu of a thinker and the "thought" he finds there contains not only commonplaces, slogans, clichés, and fashions but also serious prejudices, scientific assumptions, ideologies, and ideas of other philosophers. The stratification of all ideas and thought processes, preceding their incorporation into an original philosophy, only reveals itself to a very complex diagnosis, different for each philosophy. In order to give an idea of how a philosophy, and the whole constellation of historical philosophies, are rooted in a pre-philosophical ground, a comprehensive history of philosophy would not only have to analyze the whole series of set, current, new, old, worn-out, and forgotten ideas but also the related struggles, feelings, facts, and events. With the help of the social sciences, and through historical sources, the historian should try to reconstruct the material and cultural climate from which "the thought" (including the opinions and theoretical styles) of a period and the thought (i.e., the textually documented ideas) of individual philosophers emerged.

That various philosophers sometimes think the same thoughts can be due to a common background they share. From a philosophical perspective that is sensitive not only to historical connections but also to the originality of individual assimilation, the interesting question is: What have they made of the common elements given in their shared culture? Corresponding methods and results invite the historian to classify groups, schools, and periods. But the *life* of Philosophy is found in the inimitable *and* exemplary way in which individuals think. As soon as a philosophy becomes common property, it is levelled and worn down. The more self-evident a doctrine seems, the greater the chance that it no longer says anything. Instead of ideas springing from individuals' blood, we hear a dogmatic rhetoric urging us to believe what nobody understands anymore.

"Thinking together" is therefore not the sharing of one and the same thought process, but rather the discussion of similar problems by separate individuals within a familiar context and in mutually understood language. Loneliness and communication, the courage not to achieve conformity at any price, going one's own way of listening and discussing — all of these belong to the task of thinking. A history of philosophy must reconstruct this dimension of the collaboration and the conflict of unrepeatable thoughts.

4.8 *Historiography as a presentation of others*

Since the history of philosophy cannot be presented as one long preparation of the only true, or the best, body of thought, "true positivism" evokes the philosophers of the past and present according to their particularities. A dialogically conceived history includes common and different time-patterns, milieus, and presuppositions, as well as the unique ways in which individual thinkers have integrated those elements and confronted them.

In order to present a philosophy, I must give it every possible opportunity to be understood. My defense must show that it can remain great across time and distance. The apology for a philosophy against misunderstanding also involves protecting and strengthening it against the apologist's own philosophy. While discussing a(nother) philosopher, I must bracket my own originality. As a historian, I place myself on a metalevel "above" the community and the differences between the philosophies I present, a level above the position that I myself take as one of the many (explicit or implicit) philosophers. As a historian, I therefore stand above myself-as-philosopher.

If the writing of a history of philosophy is necessarily guided by a philosophical perspective, a historian cannot abstract altogether from his own philosophy, but he can exercise a certain *epochè* in looking at the others' thoughts "sceptically," that is, without rejecting them or subscribing to them. A similar "scepticism" is even possible towards one's own philosophy. To a certain extent I can distance myself from my convictions, make them uncertain, and look at them as a stranger. The (meta)level of this scepticism is never completely pure, since it is always bound to the first-order position that the observer occupies as philosopher. However, a clash of positions, the differences separating philosophers, also expresses their affinity in a higher, or deeper, dimension.

Aside from presenting various thinkers, a history of philosophy also explains the interrelation of their thinking. It arranges philosophical exchanges beyond the limitations of space and time. When the historian himself is an important participant in the historical debate, he has two voices: the historian allows the philosopher in him to speak — but what and how does he think as a (philosophical) historian? He has made himself a substitute for the others, and his words represent their discussions, which he has arranged. The way in which he treats the others' conversations comes from his own vision of what happens in philosophy. The more open he is, the greater the opportunity for his showing its complex dynamism. A good overview of philosophical history will abound in surprises; nothing in it will resemble a mere introduction, in praise of one system or one uniquely valid method.

The greatest difficulty in writing the history of philosophy is that while the author may not identify himself with any one philosophy, he must nevertheless understand and defend each one from a philosophical perspective and present it as philosophically relevant.

A comparison with music can perhaps elucidate the problem at hand. Ever since the nineteenth century it has been rare for great composers to be good conductors or soloists as well. A performing artist must perhaps have more distance and be less original than a creator. The historian of philosophy can be compared to the conductor who presents audiences with the products of past and present, interpreting their relations in a certain order. As "positivist," he strives for a historically correct reconstruction; as philosopher, he resurrects the dead text — a score! — so that its philosophical relevance is clearly perceptible and enjoyable, here and now. A certain *re*creating is therefore unavoidable. The positivism of historical reconstruction is only one moment of a new event, which is itself — in another cultural context — philosophical (or musical). The historian of philosophy, like a performing artist, is ruled by existing texts or scores, but these need his philosophical talent in order to rise from the dead.

Another comparison is also useful. In relating the various philosophies to one another, a historian is simultaneously judge and litigant. He determines the importance of individual philosophies and defines their constellation in the perspective of the search for truth. A judge, too, selects and collects, but he bases himself on a standard that he cannot change: the law is given by a higher power. (This schema is too simple upon closer examination, since the judge may also be forced to adjust the law according to unforeseen circumstances, but the simplified model will suffice for our purposes.) As a historian of philosophy, I have no ready-made norm from which I may judge and evaluate philosophical occurrences. The norm of philosophizing exists in the truth itself (or in the true, or "most nearly true," philosophy), and this is precisely what the historian does not have at his command. To find the truth (or more truth), he too must search, as one of many philosophers, and thus participate in the discussion on which he reports as a historian. If I believe I posses the truth, I write about the process leading to my triumph and pronounce sentence on all the others. I give up the pretension of judging all the others, however, when I carefully study each individual philosophy and stand up for it before the tribunal of my own vision of history. In this way I interpret the various philosophies as a series of experiments, repeating them myself to test their quality. I put myself in the others' places and conditionally take my chances with each of their attempts. Before I pass judgment (as a historian, I am not obliged to do so), I write the adventurous drama of the philosophical search for truth. Describing the history of philosophy, then, becomes an actual rethinking, an experimental repetition, of all the defended philosophies and their constellations — always asking: How much light do they shed? Such a history allows the reader to share in the historian's experimentation and invites him to rethink in his own way what has happened in philosophy. The final judgment is postponed until a time that nobody will ever see — because our lives are too short to perform serious and thorough experiments on the *oeuvres* of all the great creators of the past. In gloomy moments, therefore, one's inclination is to consider the writing of a history of philosophy impossible and to replace it with personal notes on a small number of texts or with a report on fortuitous visits to some high points and stages of philosophical history.

4.9 *Theatrum philosophicum*

By presenting the history of philosophical thought as a network of discussions, I arrange conversations among various philosophers without asking their permission. Most of the philosophers are not aware of my undertaking. The monological character of their works already indicates that their ideas concerning the desirability, the necessity, and the possibility of a universal dialogue are not the same as those defended here. By presenting philosophizing as a communicative constellation, I change something in the monologues I render. I summon the living and the dead and confront one with the other. But who asked me to do so? Using another image, we might say that I am a dramatist citing existing works as fragments of a dialogue, or a director setting up a role-play among the various philosophers. But who gives me this authority?

The judicial and staging power just mentioned is also exercised towards those philosophers who indeed did have explicit discussions with other philosophers. It is a historian's task to see whether Aristotle really gave a faithful rendition of Plato's ideas in his polemic against the latter, if Hegel's reproaches really do apply to the philosophies of Kant and Fichte, and so on. Many contemporaries have been ignorant of, or have ignored, one another; many others have misunderstood their colleagues. A reason for this may lie in the original style of each one's own approach, which leaves no room for the appropriation of another's approach. The distortion resulting from such a conflict creates another problem for a third party who wants to summarize the discussion between these two approaches. Not only must I reconstruct the pure doctrine of each philosopher, I must also explain *why* one distorted the other's idea and to which notion he was really opposed. It is only after such an unravelling of the factual pseudodiscussion that it becomes possible to set off a more adequate discussion between the philosophers in question, even if it is first necessary to discover a new viewpoint that neither of them saw.

Thus, a philosopher can unjustly see a caricature of his own ideas, or the expression of his own temptations, in the ideas of another. Sometimes discussions of explicit statements also conceal a profound, but unexpressed and barely conscious, incompatibility in attitude and desire. Different social milieus can greatly affect or change the meanings given to shared philosophical problems. The philosophical language and the whole approach of an original philosophy demand a certain acclamatization before one can understand it from within. To bring this kind of connection to light, the help of the psychology and sociology of thought is indispensable.

The interpretation of the history of philosophy as an ongoing discussion does not make it immune to temptations of power. For example, if I stage the whole history of philosophy just to portray my family tree (including those who made it or almost made it, and the bastards and prodigal sons or daughters), I have cleverly staged my own victory. Self-aware cultures create arches of triumph for themselves out of the ruins of the past. But a republic of letters detests dictators; it lives on the discourses of the equally unequal, who argue against each other as fairly as possible.

Whoever discovers unity in the history of philosophers and texts treats them as parts of one totality. By bringing a unified history into being, however, such a synthesis also brings it to a halt. No matter how hard I may try to keep my account open for new developments, it will inevitably have a certain completeness because these developments do not yet exist. The rendition of what has (according to this same rendition) already occurred produces a thought figure that belongs to a certain time period and a certain philosopher. It invites the reader to divide the history of thought into periods and to proceed further from the standpoint that he has reached. Every history of philosophy ties knots in the strand of time and defines a standpoint that then interrupts the continuity of philosophizing. It lends to philosophy that discontinuity necessary for true temporality. A history of philosophy is itself a contribution to the historicity of thought.

As a historian of philosophy, I have the task of realizing two desiderata simultaneously: (1) I must bring many philosophies together under one all-encompassing perspective (if this were lacking, we could speak just as little of one history as of "philosophy" in the singular); (2) I must do justice to the *uniqueness* of each of the individual philosophies and to the particular nature of their relations.

Can these two tasks be unified? Can I fulfill the first demand without overpowering many others? Even if I present my vision of philosophical history as an experiement for which I alone am responsible, I still remain the director of the laboratory where this and other philosophical experiments are being carried out.

The form of a dramatic presentation, or role-play, seems most suitable for presenting each philosophy in its uniqueness and allowing it to speak. The scene is a gathering of individuals who express themselves to one another *as others* and who enter into all kinds of relations for which they themselves are responsible. The greatness of Greek tragedy lies in the fact that the central characters are all equally justified in their actions, — hence the tragic conflict — so that no higher freedom reveals itself as a synthesis. At best, one can say that the players are sentenced by a negative power, whose wisdom — if it has any — remains hidden.

Yet even tragedy knows another superperspective: Fate. And here too the poet, just as in every drama, has supreme control of the dialogic or perspectives. Are the players not marionettes, and is the writer's overview not a restoration, at the highest (meta)level, of an all-powerful Monologue?

The organizer of the dialogue — playwright, director, or historian — has power. *He* decides who speaks and when and what is to be said. A historian of philosophy, of course, has much less leeway than a poet: he may not put words into philosophers' mouths that they did not say and would not have accepted as true renditions of their thought. His liberty is restricted to what actually exists in writing. But his selection of quotations and the personal manner in which he accentuates and interprets the others' works is a form of dominion.

As organizer of a dialogical history I lead the discussion, by allowing or preventing the others' speaking and by measuring verbal exchanges according to my own summaries and questions. My leadership is attacked if you proclaim yourself the leader of the conversation. If you have been a participant in the discussion up to that moment, you change roles: you want to take over the direction from now on. By disputing my leadership, you inaugurate a new discussion at the metalevel, at which up to now only I, as the undisputed leader, spoke. I can react to your attack in various ways: If I enter into discussion, a struggle over leadership ensues. If I react in an authoritarian manner, frustration or revolt is the outcome. If I surrender power, the same situation will arise again, with different persons taking over various roles.

Applied to our problem, all of this means that the historian of philosophy rules the discussion of philosophers from a metaviewpoint, but he is not invulnerable to dispute on the parts of those philosophers he is discussing. The dead no longer speak, but their voices resound anew when good monographies destroy the fossilized renditions that are found in average textbooks. The protest that living and dead philosophers can make to a proposed vision of their history places itself up on the metalevel mentioned and contains at least a germ of a new drama. The struggles of creative thinkers change into the struggles of those who think about them; the stage of spontaneous dialogue now becomes the dramatists' scene of battle.

The primary motive for presenting the history of philosophy as a discussion was the demand for respecting the uniqueness of every individual philosophy. But if this representation of things necessarily implies the imposing of a direction and a certain domination, does it not culminate in a final judgment and apology made by the highest judge? The historical struggles of the various philosophies would then seem to degenerate into a conversation between the judge and himself: all individuals would be moments of the "dialogue" that his soul carries on in its innermost core; his analysis of those moments would deliver a sentence that would irrevocably silence them.

Insofar as philosophy can never totally free itself from the demand that it be responsible and critical, it can never be totally free from the idea that it is a court of arbitration. But there is no concrete supreme judge whose word is law. The idea of the arbiter is the *idea* of Another who is pure and truth loving and who therefore continuously accompanies every concrete searching. A historian of philosophy is ruled, just as much as the philosophers he talks about, by the idea of a "higher" jurisdiction to which he presents his accounts. By bringing the others to speak, and by selecting texts, he sits in court, but he knows that this is merely an attempt to reveal the truth that is concealed within the various philosophies *and in their historical accounts*.

4.10 *Scepticism and time*

A good historian of philosophy invites the discussion of his history as soon as it is written. By having distanced himself from his own perspective, he knows that his staging of philosophy will be subject to criticism. He exercises a certain scepticism towards *any* attempt at writing "the history of philosophy."

Positive scepticism combines an awareness of the relativity of all philosophies and their histories with a passion for the desired truth. It does not lapse into indifference. Lacking a ready-made criterion but adverse to a dogmatic relativism, sceptical distance keeps a place open for the presentation of old and new ideas. Its freedom is undecided, engaged as it is in a series of experiments involving a multitude of philosophies. While passing from their innermost cores to their outermost limits, it tests various possible ways of understanding their differences and their unity. As soon as scepticism itself becomes a figure of consciousness, it changes into a dogma, which in turn will be conquered by other certainties. A transition from scepticism to dogmatism is inevitable, because one cannot live on a purely negative freedom that leaves everything undecided. But it will be followed by a new withdrawal, putting the dogma at a distance in order to allow for evaluation and criticism. This alternation is typical of a philosophical history that is aware of its own presuppositions. Distance and engagement are its warp and woof.

The authority to whom I present my products as a "sceptical," but not relativistic, historian is not the dogmatic scepticism just mentioned. I hope for a judge who sees some or all matters differently, and possibly better, than I do. At first it is against the concrete past and against present philosophers and historians that I can measure myself. The concrete other presents a possibility for *me* to test my own vision, as individual and as questionable. The other is the concretization of my awareness that my vision is not necessarily the true one. But factual individuals evaluating my account are not infallible either; I cannot consider them the highest, final judges of my experiment. They, too, represent individual and imperfect viewpoints — just as I do. I see them as shadows of an ideal critic: the ideal of a pure (meta)philosopher and historian, functioning as my (philosophical) conscience. The concrete other is a substitute for the utopian idea of a perfectly true evaluation of my history and philosophy.

The idea of an ideal evaluation is not achieved by the construction of an ideal society in which a universal and free communication is possible, because the absence of dominion and the equality of opportunity are not sufficient conditions for winning the truth. To what extent they are necessary conditions remains to be seen. The *social dimension* of truth should probably be understood according to a model other than that of democracy. An individual can be right without anyone else's recognizing it. To what extent is *freedom* from dominance necessary for a genuine *and true* speaking? Hegel has shown that emperor and slave can both be free and true. Is Marx correct in thinking that the proletarian's chains also bind the capitalist to a false consciousness? The ideal other is someone who has a clear insight, even if he is bound in chains and suffers social misery. The power of freedom that defies the concentration camp is more impressive than the notion of a freedom that knows no social obstacles. It is not enough for the ideal other to be free (in a way that still needs to be specified); he must also be intelligent, experienced, and skilled in philosophy. The ideal judge is a "representation accompanying the consciousness" of the philosopher; as a concrete image of his philosophical conscience, *the ideal other who knows* judges all of his products.

The supervision through which the historian of philosophy takes part in his own experiment exerts a fascination that looks ahead to the future as a time of surprises — a hope for fecund twists to all-too-well known answers. He experiences himself as one voice in a polyphonic fabric. Although his "scepticism" oversees himself as well as the others, he does not claim to have the final word. In the space kept open by his overview, all voices can be raised to speak with, and against, one another *without end*. A good philosopher dethrones himself as soon as he has erected a verbal monument. This does not mean however, that he finds his words unimportant. They are intended as a contribution to an unending conversation, which will test their force. Empirical approval or disapproval is not decisive for an answer to the question whether those words are true, but the search for truth itself forbids a philosopher to shut himself up in the loneliness of his individual (thereby, insufficient) perspective.

For both philosophy and history we can say that there is no final word; there are only provisional words, asking for replies and needing time to show their untruth or partial truth. "The truth" is not a dogma, and the deification of words is evil. Positive scepticism and inner freedom are indispensable; they do not annihilate the effort of philosophy and its history *to search* for *knowledge of the truth*. History as time is progress without end. The end of time never comes; a final judgment that completes a beginning is a historical impossibility.

4.11 *Solitude and hope*

Philosophical words are meant for others. To reach another, I need time. Will anyone take my words and do something with them on his own? The coming and going of the other (or his absence) makes up a part of the time that belongs to speaking. Philosophical speech, like all other speech, is dependent on the freedom with which others confirm its existence through replies of approval, criticism, contradiction, or development. Without another speaker's interruption to break the flow of time, a discourse loses breath. The author hopes for its prolongation, albeit by others' contradictions. Will the text procure him a little immortality?

Even if no one else hears or reads a certain text, its production is not necessarily meaningless. Even for an isolated individual, speaking before deaf ears, the act can be meaningful — for example, as a means of ordering his own thoughts, or because it is pleasurable. The hope of attracting another's attention cannot be given up, however; the possibility of an interested other is an essential condition of speaking or writing itself. As Plato says in the *Symposium*, philosophizing is an attempt to generate children in beauty. If this attempt is successful — that is, if a student develops into an independent thinker — his "father" is happy.[21] At this level, too, the desire for propagation and immortality *can* be narcissistic, but it is not necessarily so. It depends on why and with whom the desire is concerned.

No *right* exists, demanding that a philosopher be heard or answered. A reply that brings the truth closer is a gift that makes us grateful. But we cannot punish others for their indifference to our statements. If my arguments contain something important, it is a pity that my words die before they have propagated. I regret that, not only because it is a lost opportunity for others but also because, in not receiving attention, I feel neglected. The complaints of an isolated person without an audience are seldom free of resentment. But a prophet shows us that sadness can also result from disinterested efforts dedicated to great Causes.

The writings of a historian can be of great service to other philosophers. Thanks to his devotion to a past that would fade into oblivion without his efforts to keep it alive, that past — our past! — has a future. The stronger the case he makes for what was once written, the greater the chance that it can still be fruitful. Without his work the ancients' texts would lie as desiccated traces in the archives of our libraries. This history of philosophy is a commemoration, promising a future and — as long as it is taken up by others — immortality.

Chapter *IV*

Philosophy and Truth

In this book philosophy has often been defined as a search for the truth. "Truth," "the truth," and even "the truth itself" have functioned as the horizon within which philosophical activity and its history have been thematized. Even if it is not possible to analyze the "concept" of truth here thoroughly, some explanation of the presuppositions of the analyses given above seems necessary.

In chapter 3, section 4.10, the thesis was stated that all philosophizing is accompanied by the idea of an ideal evaluation, which we could call the "philosophical conscience." Philosophical thinking is a venturing of certain questions and answers, an experimental formulating aware of its own experimental and risky character. In speaking and writing as a philosopher, I must already have a certain distance from what I say; it is the beginning of a critical examination that will probably lead to a correction, and perhaps also to a radical change or a new beginning. This self-distancing critical consciousness is a nascent, vague awareness, pointing ahead towards a perfect speaking or writing that can tell the truth. The evaluating consciousness (or rather, the evaluating moment of consciousness) is not, however, the kind of knowledge that can be expressed in a statement. The peculiar nature of the accompanying "conscience" involves its remaining unsaid, prior to language. This explains its vagueness. The examining consciousness is a "knowing" that has no knowledge of objects — an "unknowing" that, like Socrates' *daimon*, is not satisfied with whatever is said; something prior to knowledge that prods me into further searching and better expression; a meta-knowledge that is impossible to concretize on the level of statements because it is the condition for their possibility. A philosopher always strives to express this "something prior to knowing" as purely as possible, but as soon as he has done it, it escapes him: it arises again behind and in front of his expressions as an unattainable horizon.

This "something prior to knowing," the "a priori" accompanying all philosophical consciousness, keeps the space for thinking open but is neither a merely negative power nor an indefinite openness. Critical examinations depend upon the standard by which one measures. The norm possessed by philosophical conscience is not a statement, but rather something that precedes all statements and indicates their goal: the good of philosophy — that is, the truth. If philosophy were the highest, this goal would also be the greatest of all goods: το ἀγαθον καθ' αὑτο.

Something unsaid and unsayable, which regulates all statements, a standard of formulated truth, which itself cannot be put into words — is this not "magic" or "mystical" nonsense? Many attempts at naming this unsayable unsaid are known in the history of philosophy: The One, the Thing-in-itself, the Absolute, Spirit, Substance, Idea, αὑτο το ὀν, *ipsum Esse* or Being itself — all these names have referred to the horizon towards which philosophy moves, without ever being able to attain it. To indicate something without knowing and saying it — is this possible? Yes, it is, if all saying is itself animated by a movement pointing beyond all words; if life and thought receive their ultimate meaning from something that itself cannot be captured in one of our "categories."

The experience of thinking referred to here — the tension between the practice of verbal experiments and the nonverbal "conscience" with which this practice tries to coincide — corresponds to the way in which we experience moral, aesthetic, and religious realities. Perhaps a similar tension is characteristic of all types of experience. The enjoyment of a piece of music, for example, or the perception of the world as a domain inhabited by gods, is an experience in which the affirmation of a certain fullness (or "fulfillment") does not exclude, but rather includes, a critical evaluation of its own quality. Since such experiences are always, at least in some respects, imperfect, their self-evaluation urges us to search beyond them for a more adequate experience. Aside from satisfaction and rest, experience is also the beginning of self-criticism. Although I come to know reality by enjoying it, I do not stop at the aspects of reality that I have discovered. Authentic experience relativizes the involvement into which it has drawn me. Every appreciation is mixed with shadows of unfulfillment. A static definition of experience neglects the fact that the experiencing subject is driven towards greater experiential adequacy.

For each of the areas mentioned — morality, art, religion, and philosophy — and perhaps for all areas of culture, it is possible to sketch a suitable route description, or methodology, based on the typical paths of experience characterizing them. For the ways and movements of experience are characterized by a certain structure and regularity. Thus, a preliminary sketch of the "method" of philosophy can distinguish the following moments:

a. The entirety of an individual search may be seen as the construction of a path under the direction, and in "light," of a desire for truth, involving a kind of "foreknowledge" of this goal and the direction towards it.

b. Traveling this path means venturing certain expressions, intended as suitable formulations of reality. The journey cannot even begin if I shrink away from all imperfect formulations, but it ends prematurely if I make my experiment into a dogma.

c. Under the influence of the guiding "(un)knowing" (which gives "more light", but not more knowledge, beyond what is said), I discover that what I have said up to this point is unsatisfactory. This discovery may express itself either in a suspicion or in an obscure certainty. But as a thinker, I will make every effort to find out exactly where my shortcoming lies and to formulate it precisely.

d. In becoming conscious of my errors, I may experience a crisis. If my errors are only logical inconsistencies, an incorrect working out of certain principles, I try to correct my text, but its foundations remain intact. Much more serious, and also more fruitful, is the discovery of a fundamental mistake that forces me to change my ideas radically. There are many philosophical schools and individuals who have never suffered a fundamental crisis. Their dogmatism expresses itself in pedantic "self-evidences" or naive praises of unassailable logics, but their apparent self-assurance (a sort of blinding) is a reward for their superficiality. A philosopher who tries to think radically (a tautology!) takes the great chance of undermining his own thought.

e. Obliged by my failures to face my fundamental mistakes, I am forced to look for a radically new possibility of thought. A new phase in my thinking begins, if I have the strength to risk another hypothesis that is more promising than the previous one. Because it has sprung from a crisis with my very foundations, this new attempt is not a conclusion, but a leap. This kind of discontinuity, resulting from a leap, generates a philosophical *history*. The working out of hypotheses does not generate new events but constitutes a temporal continuity.

The right attitude, and the right opportunity, help a thinker to progress in the direction of the truth. This has been the presupposition of our discussion on an approach to "the truth." To speak of "more" or "less" of the truth would be meaningless if the *thought* of a perfect truth were (a) senseless and (b) not the goal and norm of thinking. Under "truth" we must then understand: a thinking or speaking that says and thinks "what is," what is "going on," or what, and how, reality is (doing). (The demand to *begin* with an ambiguous definition is unjustified, because it already *implies* an entire theory of truth.) What "reality as it really is" means, and how it is possible to use such an expression, is — certainly at first — not clear. To avoid any misunderstanding it is important to point out that "reality" cannot be adequately differentiated out of the speaking in which it is put into words: it includes not only people and things but also all statements concerning reality, all philosophies, cultures, and histories. "Reality" is also a *thought*, to wit, of something all-inclusive, including not only the actual people, things, words, and histories but, equally, all possibilities of the past and present. To say that thought should *for this reason* "be only a thought and thus no (real) reality" is an incorrect conclusion. Perhaps the coinciding of this thought (or "idea") with the all-inclusive (authentic or "true") reality is the ideal and the prototype of all truth. Perhaps truth must be "defined" as the identity of a thought together with the reality that is intended by this thought.

Of course, reality is not accessible to thought that is separated from thinking. As a thinker I cannot place myself outside my own thinking to affirm or deny the adequacy of this same thinking towards reality — unless "thinking" itself is *double*: a "categorical" thinking that expresses itself in statements and a "transcendental" thinking that accompanies the former and sees (by transcendental inspection or "skepsis") whether it satisfies the ideal of truth, which the thinker has somehow projected, without getting a definitive grip on it. The transcendental "thinking," or (fore)knowledge, refers categorical thinking to the truth and points a way out of the statements that imprison and break the truth.

In the section devoted to a positive kind of scepticism (4.10), truth is presented in the image of the highest, and thus the ideal, judgment; the context perhaps suggests that such a judgment might correspond to the sentence of an ideal judge. The complete truth, however, cannot rest in an individual thinking, because — even if it is pure — it is necessarily perspectivized and made one-sided by its individuality. On the basis of the relativity of all philosophies, this book has defended an irrevocable (but not relativistic) pluralism, while both philosophy and its history have been interpreted as an unending dialogue. "The truth" is never the property of one philosopher, who can judge all the others. Truth comes to be out of the interplay between the various philosophical constellations. Not as though the history of philosophy were a gradual construction of the one and the whole truth, however, because such a notion presupposes a clandestine spirit's using history as an instrument for the gradual building up of its most adequate knowledge, or a History that is itself Providence. How could a human being reveal the plan of this providence if he did not himself coincide with it? The actual production of (more or less) truth by philosophy in the course of its history forms a contingent constellation, which could also have turned out differently — unless one could prove that all the stages of its factual evolution have been a necessary unfolding of the preceding ones. If a philosophy of history could carry out such a proof, with reference to all known philosophers, it would abolish all discontinuity and present all thinkers as moments in the continuous unfolding of one initial thought.

The intersubjective dimension of philosophizing is presented in this book as a (relative) victory over the relativism of *perspectivity*. Discussion is "the place of truth." But it is not a panacea, and *itself not the highest norm*. Just as the one complete definitive judgment cannot be found in an ideal individual, neither can it issue from a learned forum or a gathering of judges who reach agreement or force a decision.

Neither intersubjectivity nor communication can replace the norm of the truth, since individual thoughts and statements are themselves ruled by this norm. That some people define truth in terms of "domination-free communication" can be explained, I believe, by the combination of a relativistic despair over the possibility of reaching any ("objective") truth on the one hand and an application of the democratic model to thinking on the other. They defend democratization of the truth by treating theoretical questions and methods as if they were political problems and strategies.

By defining truth as a certain number of coherent statements subscribed to by everyone, if all thinkers could confer with one another in a nonviolent situation, one at least shows that the production of truth presupposes freedom from violence and consensus (which must be specified further). Neither of the two conditions is self-evident, however. If those who refer to a possible consensus merely intend to state their expectation that an empirical agreement will be the result, and thus a sign, of truths that cannot reasonably be denied, then their definition will appeal to a particular notion of truth that precedes this consensus and includes a utopian optimism about the convincing force of truth. If consensus were really intended as an element of the definition, it could only be conceived as an ascertainable or predictable *fact*. By presenting consensus as something *demanded* by human reason (and not as an unavoidable occurrence), one again appeals to a normative notion of truth and stresses its total independence of any factual consensus.

Why should consensus be a necessary condition, or even an element, of truth? Even if we admit that freedom from external coercion is a necessary condition for true knowledge, this condition is insufficient to enable all the participants in the debate to reach the same insight — which may be called "true." If this is the case at the level of everyday practical wisdom and common sense, it is even more so at the level of philosophy, which presupposes expertise in an extremely difficult field. Some people are dull; others are intelligent, but unsuited for philosophy: Nobel prize winners sometimes utter philosophical nonsense. Aside from intellectual "virtues," the search for truth demands other qualities — and here we come to an argument concerning freedom from violence. Not only the presentation of true insights, but their conception as well, can demand great courage. The freedom necessary for true thoughts and statements depends primarily on an ability to resist the external and internal forces that drive us in the wrong direction. We do not know exactly how much protection from societal violence is necessary to allow free thinking and writing. But we do not have to wait for a utopian and illusory situation, granting complete freedom from restraint. For how could we then criticize the current situation, here and now? If a theory of truth refers us to the future of a successful democratic discussion, it must know a great deal about the truth and its relation to freedom and society. It leaves the responsibility for true knowledge up to the society, which supposedly hinders the production of truth here and now. But true knowledge is not only *demanded* here and now; it is *possible* as well, if individuals are unselfish enough to aim beyond their own particularism towards what is valid for all, without necessarily being recognized by everyone. All genuine philosophers would be grateful if some kind of liberation made it easier for everybody to remain independent of powers and fashions, so that we would not replace one ideology with another but could criticize all of them. Such a liberation would *perhaps* be an empirical condition for a genuine democratization of philosophy. It is not a condition, however, but a consequence of the truth that some — the best, an elite — now understand.

A theory that identifies truth with the consensus resulting from an ideal dialogue has no means of evaluating the quality of such a consensus. Democracy is not a remedy for the conspiracies of wily sophists. A situation in which everyone receives an equal chance seems, in fact, more suitable for conflicts and tragedies. "The truth" is not beloved by all and is known only to a few of her intelligent lovers, and then only in part. But even if one admits that the kind of "freedom" intended here certainly produces truth, the theory cannot say how such an ideal consensus is related to reality and why it still uses the word *truth*. Is the issue here not peace, and the equality of opportunity, rather than discourse telling us what the facts are and what actually goes on? Besides being democratic, such a theory is also pacifistic. For fear of struggle? Yet struggles against internal egotism, particularism, and lack of freedom cannot be delegated to others, or to society. Truthseeking is much more polemic than the theory of an actual or desired consensus can imagine.

Does the qualitative, "elitist," and aggressive notion of truthseeking argued for in this book not testify to an authoritarian contempt for the vulgar herd? One is best protected against this by the impersonal norm of the ideal evaluation given by truth itself, not by the dictatorship of a "collective." A good elite (allowing this pleonasm here) keeps places open for dissidents in the search for truth, even if their voices are scarcely audible amidst the deafening, and soporific, disputation of all against all. It has happened that "the truth" was on the side of the exceptions and met its death with theirs. Later they were commemorated as heroes of the truth, but the popularization or democratization of their message cannot take the place of our own thinking. The authority of the best lies in the degree to which they provide others with food for thought. Since authentic thought is independent, the best thinkers are good as long as they make others ever freer to discuss things with the best and with each other. Up to the present time, the history of philosophy has been a history of several *aristoi* and their schools. Not everyone must become a philosopher, but the only ground for exclusion lies in the prerequisites that the nature of philosophical thinking involves. Aside from a love of truth, facility in language and reflection are also necessary — skills that are not yet universally possessed. A philosophical people's democracy, then, seems Utopian. It is a pity that many will always be denied the quality and enjoyment provided by philosophy, and it is a loss for philosophy that many individuals cannot bring their perspectives and styles into the philosophical debate. But even if they could, philosophy would still not be an all-encompassing truth. The collection of those who participate in the history of philosophy remains as fortuitous as the stellar constellations in the heavens. The number of participants does not change this; even the collection of *all* people would be a contingency. The rise, and movements, of philosophical constellations deserve admiration and stimulate thinking. Their contingency does not hinder their being perceived and connected as figures within one all-inclusive whole. The exciting thing about history is that new perspectives can always emerge. As attempts at overarching, all philosophies and all histories of philosophy are phenomena that can change the firmament. Even metaphilosophies and methodologies of philosophy do not come any further than one aspect of or variation in the starry sky. But, is that not enough?

Notes

1. It is the *Bibliografisch Repertorium* (also published as the *Répertoire bibliographique de la philosophie*) of the *Tijdschrift voor Filosofie* and of the *Revue Philosophique de Louvain* that is referred to here. In pp. 96–99 of my *Weefsels* (Weavings: Bilthoven: Ambo, 1974) a short overview (and commentary is given) of the titles found in that Repertory during the years 1970–72. The situation has probably changed little since 1972.

2. This difference between a philosopher and one who knows philosophy is illuminated in *Weefsels* 12ff. and 99–100.

3. Cf. E. Gilson, *Etudes sur le rôle de la pensée médiévale dans la formation du système cartésien*, 2d. ed (Paris, 1951) and *Index scolastico-cartésien*, 2d. ed. (Paris , 1979).

4. A thesis to be thematized below, which already plays a role here, holds that the most radical perspective of every concrete thinking is precisely the (simultaneously contingent and necessary) fact of its individuality, which makes it unique and unrepeatable, without losing its universality.

5. Cf. G.W.F. Hegel: "Uneducated people enjoy reasoning and placing blame, for blame is easy to find, but it is difficult to know its (i.e., a philosophy's) goodness and inner necessity. Education always begins with blame, but when completed, it sees the positive in everything." *Grundlinien der Philosophie des Rechts* (Berlin, 1820), addition to §268.

6. As Jacques Derrida believes and brilliantly exemplifies.

7. A philosophical analysis of the learning process can be found in *Weefsels*, 47–62 and 148–156.

8. Cf. Plato, *Phaedrus*, 247b–277a and the seventh letter; cf. also E. Levinas, *Totalité et infini* (The Hague: Nijhoff, 1961), 45, 69–71; *Totality and Infinity*, trans. A. Lingis (Pittsburgh-The Hague: Nijhoff, 1969), 72–73, 96–98.

9. Cf. Plato, *Sophist*, 263e4-264a9.

10. Cf. my "Philosophical Introductions and Pluralism." *Metaphilosophy* 16 (1985): 250-259.

11. An analysis of the human battle hinted at in the following pages can be found in *U en ik* (You and I). See *U en Ik* (Bilthoven: Ambo, 1975), 47-68.

12. Ἀγαθὴ ἔρις were the opening words of my school song at the Municipal *Gymnasium* in Hilversum, which I have to thank for my initiation into Graeco-European civilization; here I acquired my first love for Plato's *oeuvre*.

13. Cf. *U en ik*, 11-28, 47-51.

14. Cf. E. Levinas, *Totalité et infini*, 54-78; *Totality and Infinity*, 82-105.

15. Cf. *U en ik*, 63-65, 74-75, 95-99.

16. Cf. for the following also H. Kuhn, "Ideologie als hermeneutischer Begriff" (Ideology as a hermeneutic concept). *Hermeneutik und Dialektik* I (1970),: 343-356.

17. Cf. S. IJsseling, *Retoriek en Filosofie: Wat gebeurt er wanneer er gesproken wordt?* (Rhetoric and Philosophy). Bilthoven: Ambo, 1975; 128.

18. Cf. the whole *oeuvre* of E. Levinas, especially *Autrement qu'être ou au-delà de l'essence* (Otherwise than Being or Beyond Essence), and passages such as: *Totalité et Infini*, 54-55, 217-225, 278-284 (Totality and Infinity, 82-83, 240-247, 302-307). Cf. also "Beyond Being. Emmanuel Levinas: Autrement qu'être ou au-delà de l'essence; The Hague: Nijhoff 1974." *Research in Phenomenology* VIII (1978): 239-261.

19. Cf. my *Vrijheid* (Freedom). Bilthoven: Ambo, 1975; 37-42.

20. Cf. Plato, *Phaedrus*, 274b-277a and E. Levinas, *Totalité et Infini*, 45, 69, 71; Totality and Infinity, 73, 96, 98.

21. Cf. Plato, *Symposium*, 206b-209e.

Selected Bibliography

Alquié, F. "Structures logiques et structures mentales en histoire de la philosophie." *Bulletin de la société française de philosophie* 46–47 (1952–53): 89–107.

_____ . "Intention et déterminations dans la genèse de l'oeuvre philosophique." In *Philosophie et méthode*, Bruxelles: Editions de l'université de Bruxelles, 1974. 28–42.

Armstrong, A.M., "Philosophy and its History." *Philosophy and Phenomenological Research* 19 (1958–59): 447–465.

Beck, L. J. "Progrès et philosophie." In *Etudes sur l'histoire de la philosophie*, Paris: Fischbacher, 1964. 115–126.

Beck, L. W. "Introduction and Bibliography." *The Monist 53* (1969): 523–531.

Belaval, Y. "Continu et discontinu en histoire de la philosophie." In: *Philosophie et Méthode*, 75–84. Bruxelles: Editions de l'université de Bruxelles, 1974.

Braun, L. *Histoire de l'histoire de la philosophie*. Paris: Ophrys, 1973.

Bréhier, E. "Introduction." In: *Histoire de la philosophie*, Vol. I, 1–37. Paris: Presses Universitaires de France, 1943.

Brelage, M. "Die Geschichtlichkeit der philosophie und die Philosophiegeschichte." *Zeitschrift für philosophische Forschung* 16 (1962): 375–405.

Bruch, J. L. "Le philosophe et son lecteur." In *Études sur l'histoire de la philosophie*, 213–223. Paris: Fischbacher, 1964.

Brunner, F. "Histoire de la philosophie et philosophie." Ibid., 179–204.

Butler, J. F. "Some Epistemological Problems about the History of Philosophy." *Philosophical Quarterly* (Amalner, India) 22 (1949–50): 125–135.

Châtelet, F. "La question de l'histoire de la philosophie aujourd'hui." In *Politiques de la philosophie*, edited by D. Grisoni, 31–53. Paris: Grasset, 1976.

Collins, J. *Interpreting Modern Philosophy*. Princeton: Princeton University Press, 1972.

Copleston, F. "On the History of Philosophy." In F. Copleston, *On the History of philosophy and other Essays*. London: Search Press, 1979.

Duméry, H. "Doctrine et structure." In *Études sur l'histoire de la philosophie*, 155–176. Paris: Fischbacher, 1964.

Dunn, J. "The Identity of the History of Ideas." *Philosophy* 42 (1968): 85–104.

Ehrhardt, W. *Philosophiegeschichte und geschichtlicher Skeptizismus. Untersuchungen zur Frage: Wie ist Philosophiegeschichte möglich?* München: Francke, 1957.

Ehrlich, W. *Philosophie der Geschichte der Philosophie*. Tübingen: Niemeyer, 1965.

———. "Principles of a Philosophy of the History of Philosophy." *The Monist* 53 (1969): 532–562.

Faurot, J.N. "What is History of Philosophy?" *The Monist 53* (1969): 642–655.

Feibleman, J. K. "The History of Philosophy as a Philosophy of History." *Southern Journal of Philosophy* 5 (1967): 375–383.

Flach, W. "Die Geschichtlichkeit der Philosophie und der Problemcharakter des philosophischen Gegenstandes." *Kant-Studien* 54 (1963): 17–28.

Gadamer, H. G. *Wahrheit und Methode; Grundzüge einer philosophischen Hermeneutik*. 3d ed. Tübingen Mohr, 1972.

Garin, E. "L' unità nella storiografia filosofica." *Rivista critica di storia della filosofia* 11 (1956): 206–217.

———. "Osservazioni preliminari a una storia della filosofia." *Giornale critica della filosofia italiana* 38 (1959): 1–52 (Discussion by G. Saitta and others: pp. 353–407).

———. "Ancora della storia della filosofia e del suo metodo." Ibid., 39 (1960): 373–390, 521–535.

Geldsetzer, L. *Was heisst Philosophiegeschichte?* Düsseldorf: Philosophia Verlag, 1968.

———. *Die Philosophie der Philosophiegeschichte im 19. Jahrhundert*. Meisenheim a. G.: Hain 1968.

Gilson, E. *History of Philosophy and Philosophical Education*. Milwaukee: Marquette University Press 1948.

Goldschmidt, V. "Remarques sur la méthode structurale en histoire de la philosophie. In *Metaphysique, Histoire de la philosophie*. Recueil d'études offert à Fernand Brunner, 213-240. Neuchâtel: La Baconnière, 1981.

Goldschmidt, W. "Die Aufgaben des Philosophie-Historikers. Eine analytische Studie." *Zeitschrift für philosophische Forschung* 9 (1955): 581-613.

Gouhier, H. *La philosophie et son histoire*. Paris: Vrin, 1944.

_____. "Vision rétrospective et intention historique." In *La philosophie de l'histoire de la philosophie*. Edited by E. Castelli, Paris: Vrin, 1956. 133-142.

_____. "Note sur le progrès et la philosophie." In *Études sur l'histoire de la philosophie*, 111-115. Paris: Fischbacher, 1964.

_____. "La philosophie et ses publics." In *Philosophie et methode*, 61-74. Bruxelles: Éditions de l'université de Bruxelles, 1974.

_____, Y. Belaval, Lefebvre, Croissant, Van Steenberghen, Serres, Robinet. *Philosophie et méthode*. Bruxelles: Editions de l'université de Bruxelles.

Graham, G. "Can there be History of Philosophy?" *History and Theory* 21 (1982): 37-52.

Granger, G. G. "Systèmes philosophiques et métastructures. L' argumentation du tractatus." In *Études sur l'histoire de la philosophie*, 139-154. Paris: Fischbacher, 1964.

_____. "L'histoire comme analyse des oeuvres et comme analyse des situations." In *Médiations* I, (1961), 127-142.

Guéroult, M. "Le problème de la légitimité de l'histoire de la philosophie." In *La philosophie de l'histoire de la philosophie*. Edited by E. Castelli, 45-68. Paris: Vrin, 1956.

_____. "The History of Philosophy as a Philosophical Problem." *The Monist* 53 (1969): 563-587.

_____. "La méthode en histoire de la philosophe," in *Philosophie et Méthode*, 17-27, Bruxelles: Editions de l'université de Bruxelles, 1974.

_____. *Dianoématique*. Livre I: *Histoire de l'histoire de la philosophie* I: *En Occident, des origines jusqu' à Condillac*. Paris: Aubier, 1984. Livre II: *Philosophie de l'histoire de la philosophie*. Paris: Aubier, 1979.

Karskens, M. "Tussen geschiedenis en filosofie. Aantekeningen rond enige problemen van de geschiedenis van de filosofie." *Wijsgerig Perspektief op maatschappij en wetenschap* 21 (1980-81): 70-76.

Kristeller, P. O. "The Philosophical Significance of the History of Thought." *Journal of the History of Ideas* 7 (1946): 360-366. (Also in P. O. Kristeller. *Studies in Renaissance Thought and Letters*. Roma: Edizioni di Storia e Letteratura, 1956).

———. "History of Philosophy and History of Ideas," *Journal of the History of Philosophy* 2 (1964): 1-14.

Lefebvre, H. "La métaphilosophie devant l'histoire de la philosophie." In *Philosophie et mèthode*, 85-89. Bruxelles: Editions de l'université de Bruxelles, 1974.

von Leyden, W. "Philosophy and its History." *Proceedings of the Aristotelian Society* 54 (1953-54): 187-208.

Lombardi, F. ed. *Verità e storia. Un dibattito sullo metodo della storia della filosofia*. Asti: Arethusa, 1956.

Lovejoy, A. O. "Introduction. The Study of the History of Ideas." In *The Great Chain of Being*. Cambridge, Mass.: Harvard University Press, 1936.[1]

Mandelbaum, M. "History of Ideas, Intellectual History and History of Philosophy." *History and Theory*, Beiheft 5 (1965). 33-66.

———. "On the Historiography of Philosophy." *Philosophy Research Archives* II (1976).

———. "The History of Philosophy; Some Methodological Issues." *The Journal of Philosophy* 74 (1977): 561-572.

Mittelstrass, J. "Das Interesse der Philosophie an ihrer Geschichte." *Studia Philosophica* 36 (1976): 3-15.

Nash, R. H., ed. *Ideas of History*: Vol I. *Speculative Approaches to History*. Vol. II: *The Critical Philosophy of History*. New York: Dutton, 1969.

Nelson, L. "What is History of Philosophy?" *Ratio* 4 (1962): 22-35.

del Noce, A. "Problèmes de la périodisation historique." In *La philosophie de l'histoire de la philosophie*, Edited by E. Castelli, 143-168. Paris: Vrin, 1956.

Oehler, K. "Die Geschichtlichkeit der Philosophie." *Zeitschrift für philosophische Forschung* 11 (1957): 504-526.

———. "Der Entwicklungsgedanke als heuristisches Prinzip der Philosophiegeschichte." *Zeitschrift für philosophische Forschung* 17 (1963): 604-613.

Passmore, P. "The Idea of a History of Philosophy," *History and Theory* Beiheft 5 (1965): 1-32.

_____. "Historiography of Philosophy." *Encyclopedia of Philosophy* (1967), VI: 226–230.

Peperzak, A. "On the Unity of Systematic Philosophy and the History of Philosophy." In *Against Anti-History in Philosophy.* Edited by V. Tejera & T. Lavine. To be published by M. Nyhoff, The Hague, in 1986.)

Randall, J. N. *How Philosophy Uses its Past.* New York: Colombia University Press, 1963.

Reé, J., M. Ayers, A. Westboy, eds. *Philosophy and its Past.* Hassocks: The Harvester Press, 1978.

Ricoeur, P. "L' histoire de la philosophie et l'unité du vrai," In P. Ricoeur, *Histoire et verité*, 45–59. Paris: Du Seuil, 1955.

_____. "Histoire de la philosophie et historicité." Ibid., 66–80.

_____. "Qu'est-ce qu'un texte? Expliquer et comprendre," In *Hermeneutik und Dialektik*, 181–200. Tübingen: Mohr, 1970.

Ritzel, W. "Die Philosophie und ihre Geschichte." *Zeitschrift für philosophische Forschung* 11 (1957): 235–251.

Rorty, R., J.B. Schneewind, Q. Skinner, eds. *Philosophy in History; Essays on the historiography of philosophy.* Cambridge: Cambridge University Press, 1984.

Santinello, G., ed. *Storia delle storie generali della filosofia*, Vol I: *Dalle origini rinascimentali alla "historia philosophica."* Vol II: *Dall' età cartesiana a Brucker.* Brescia: La Scuola, 1981 & 1979.

Sass, H. M. "Philosophische Positionen in der Philosophiegeschichts-schreibung." *Deutsche Vierteljarhrsschrift für Literaturwissenschaft und Geistesgeschichte* 46 (1972): 539–567.

Sebba, G. "What is 'History of Philosophy'?" *Journal of the History of Philosophy* 8 (1970): 251–252.

Smart, H. R. *Philosophy and its History.* La Salle: Open Court, 1963.

Tonelli, G. "Qu'est-ce que l'histoire de la philosophie?" *Revue philosophique de la France et de l'Etranger* 152 (1962): 290–306.

_____. "A Contribution towards a Bibliography on the Methodology of the History of Philosophy." *Journal of the History of Philosophy* 10 (1972): 456–458 (additions to the bibliography of L. W. Beck in *The Monist* 53 [1969]).

Voelke, A.J. "La fonction heuristique de la tradition en philosophie." *Studia Philosophica* 36 (1976): 15–24.

Wiener, P. P. "Some Problems and Methods in the History of Ideas." *Journal of the History of Ideas* 22 (1961): 531–548.

Wimmer, F. M. "Philosophiegeschichtsschreibung in praktischer Absicht." *Conceptus* 14 (1980): 28–46.

See also the bibliographical selections given by Beck (1969), Braun, Bréhïer, Geldsetzer (*19. Jahrhundert*), Karskens (1980–81), Mandelbaum (1965), Passmore (1965 & 1967), Sass (1972), and Tonelli (1972).

Index of Proper Names

Subject Index

167

as, 103–105; time structure of, 102–103. *See also* discussion, listening, polemic, rhetoric, speaking.
counterviolence, 91–95. *See also* violence, antiviolence.
court of justice, 34. *See also* history of philosophy.
crisis, 3, 7, 92, 150
criticism, 15, 37–38, 84, 86, 89, 112–113, 118, 148; absolutizing of, 112; as beginning of learning, 14; self-criticism, 96, 112, 147
culture, 30

daimon, 147
death, 23
decline, 134
defeatism, 68
democracy in philosophy, 25, 98–101, 153–154
democratization of culture, 40; of philosophy, 153; of truth, 152, 154
demystification, 55, 57
desire, 111
determinism, 118–119
diagnosis, 3
dialogue, 72–86; history of philosophy as, 134, 141; *versus* oeuvre, 104; philosophical, 25, 72; philosophy as, 107, 115; search of truth as, 99; of the soul with itself, 142; therapeutic significance of, 96. *See also* conversation.
discussion, 80, 97–99; as element of every dialogue, 87; history of philosophy as, 105, 129–132; between master and pupil, 72, 78; of basic perspectives, 26, 90, 139; philosophy as, 105; as place of the truth, 152; as struggle, 141. *See also* conversation, dialogue, dispute, rhetoric, violence.
disputatio, 98
dispute, 88
distortion, 139

dogma, 72, 129, 144, 149
dogmatism, 68, 134, 149
doxa, 129

education, 91–95
ego, 14, 26, 119, 125. *See also* I.
egology, 24, 25, 71, 116, 125
elite, 154
emancipation, 13–14, 131
emotion, 92
empirical, 129
empiricism, 10
enmity, 60
epigone, 10, 28, 69, 85, 127, 128, 133, 134
epochè, 136
equality, 87
ethics, 91, 115, 119; of interpretation, 124–126; of polemics, 93–96; of violence, 91–93
evaluation, 125, 143, 147; self-evaluation, 148
everyman, 132
evidence, 117, 149
exegete, 10, 122
exodus, 65
experience, 53; authentic, 128, 149; as experiment, 55; fundamental, 56; and philosophy, 53–56, 57; self-experience, 118, 128; thinking as, 148
experiment, 21, 55, 138, 140, 149
experimentation, 138
expertise, 133

faith, 128
fashion, 14, 32, 33, 36, 37
fate, 140
fecundity, 29
feeling, 111, 117
Fernstenliebe, 90
force, 97, 101, 114, 118. *See also* power, violence.
form, 11, 83, 84.
formalism, 4, 16–18